THE CHÂTEAUX OF THE LOIRE
AND THEIR SURROUNDINGS

TEXT
GILLES DU PONTAVICE

PHOTOGRAPHS
RICHARD VOLANTE

TRANSLATION: 5/5

Éditions Ouest-France

INTRODUCTION

« THE LOIRE, a vast river of sand in which flows a little water. »

Throughout this book, we will seek to prove this disabused comment from Jules Renard wrong. As we explore the « last wild river of Europe », and the rivers that flow into it, we will travel both upstream and back in time. Taking the time to make a stop before beautiful residences, which are countless in their numbers ; and also the time to sample the many tasty products ; and to quench our thirst for the fine wines of the Loire, which are plentiful.

As we drift along with the flow, I will tell you about the Loire's great history and small stories. I will tell you about René of Anjou, the king of Jerusalem, and Dédé de Luché, the king of the « boule de Fort ». I will describe one hundred and fifty châteaux and castles for you, from the most famous edifices to small, forgotten manor houses. I will, I hope, make you want to taste each of the forty wines and one thousand recipes from the Loire. And, since this is the purpose of this book, I will try to awaken in you the irresistible desire to saunter along roads, from the Anjou to the Sancerrois, in search of all that I may have forgotten to mention.

Jules Renard is, as always, quite right : there is more than just water in the Loire. There is also the sand and the stone with which so many châteaux and villages have been built over the last thousand years.

The Angevin Loire

From Angers to Saumur, the Angevin Loire remembers the court of king René, the duke of Anjou, but also king of Naples and Jerusalem... The county of Anjou was created in the 10th century in an effort to contain the Norman invaders, who had for many years been launching raids along the Loire.

One of the first counts of Anjou was Foulques Nerra the Black (972-1040), a tireless warrior who fought battles in the regions of the Mauges, Touraine, and the Vendômois... He was also a great builder, whose formidable keeps are scattered throughout the country. He did, however, destroy many others!

With Geoffrey Plantagenêt, the Anjou passed into the hands of the English, and was then united to the crown of France. It is between 1356, when Jean Le Bon created the duchy of Anjou for the benefit of his youngest son Louis, and 1481, when the duchy was returned to the insatiable Louis XI, that the counts of Anjou became kings... without ever gaining

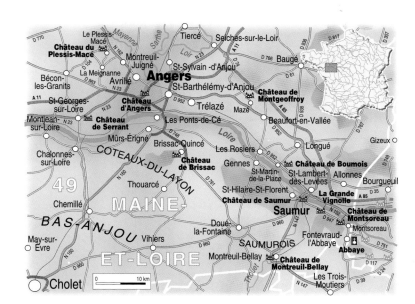

access to their respective thrones. The castle of Angers, with its levelled towers, is well and truly the symbol of this shattered destiny.

The château of Brissac

The duke of Brissac will soon celebrate the fifth centenary of his family's presence in these walls. From the old castle of the Brézé family, Brissac has gradually risen to seven floors : "A new château that is built to a half, in an old castle that is destroyed to a half." The 17th century mansion rises between the old towers. Some rooms are monumental, like the kitchen and the guards room, both thirty-two metres in length. But one also finds here a bedroom that witnessed, in 1620, the reconciliation of king Louis XIII with his mother Marie de Médicis. And even, on the second floor, a theatre that was inaugurated in 1890. Indeed, the Brissac family, soldiers and regular visitors to the house of the kings of France, also gave us poets and writers. Nowadays, they devote themselves to their richly furnished château and the red Anjou vineyard that surrounds it.

The château of Serrant

More of a palace than a château, Serrant has travelled through centuries without sustaining any damage, since the time of its construction in 1546, on the remains of a stronghold. Further works did not disfigure its sober façade, on which the ornamentation is concentrated at the level of the dormers. It presents similarities with Valençay, Villandry and Chenonceau. The interior is richly furnished, and its library is impressive. All in all, a vast and beautiful mansion, in which several rooms are open to visits, rooms which have welcomed Louis XIV and both the emperors.

At the feet of this castle run the river Maine and the motorway to Paris. Sometimes, the Maine, in anger, floods the motorway; the opposite, fortunately, never happens. All around, the city is alternately comprised of old districts and wealthy streets.

Angers has a fine history of liqueurs: here was created the "menthe-pastille", alcohol with peppermint, which is known to help digestion. And the Gui-

The Loire in Angers.

gnolet too, an aperitif cherry liqueur; the company that produces it was founded in 1849 by the Cointreau family. A heir, Louis Cointreau, first prepared, in 1875, the liqueur that now still bears his name. This liqueur is made with oranges; to produce it, 260 tons of bitter orange skins are imported from the Caribbean every year,

as well as 1,000 tons of sweet orange skins, which come from the Mediterranean basin; the other production steps are a jealously kept secret.

The richness of Angers lies beyond its walls: in times past, this richness was slate, that of Angers and Trélazé, whose prestige remains, even if Spanish slate imports have dealt it a severe blow. The Blue Mine is a descent into space and time: 130 metres below the ground, one discovers the world of the slate miners.

The vineyard is, on the other hand, alive and well, and has experienced, over the past ten years, quite an upturn. Every year, at the end of January, Angers welcomes the "Salon des vins de Loire" (*the*

Loire wine Fair), drawing a crowd of wine merchants from all around the world. This is when the "Liger" awards are presented, to reward the finest vintages of

The château of Le Plessis-Macé

The pleasant composite courtyard of the château of Le Plessis-Macé is an anthology of Renaissance architecture: corbelled stair turret, flamboyant style chapel, finely carved doors and windows. One may recall that it long belonged to the du Bellay family, which gave birth to a famous poet of the Loire. However, the imposing ruins of the great 15th century square keep are a reminder of rather more troubled times : arrow slits are still to be seen next to the large Renaissance windows.

each appellation of the Loire's vineyards *(Translator's note: An "appellation contrôlée" is a label of quality guaranteeing the origin of the wine. "Appellations" are also applied to a certain number of French cheeses).*

Old incidents around customs duties, in which Dutch wine merchants have been found to play a rather active part, prompted the Anjou vineyards to begin growing the Chenin Blanc, a vine produ-

The castle of Angers

This was a formidable fortress, worthy of its builders. Foulques Nerra first, who raised as many castles as he destroyed! Then Saint Louis, who raised the castle walls: seventeen towers rising to heights of forty metres. The dukes of Anjou continued further with the constructions : abode, chapel, gate house. In 1375, Louis I ordered a tapestry that would match the castle's excessiveness, and that depicted Saint John's Apocalypse. In the times of the good king René, duke of Anjou but also king of Sicily and of Jerusalem (although his crown remained theoretical in every respect), feasts were given continuously, and Angers was a capital of arts and literature.

In 1481, the Anjou region and the castle were united to the royal domain by Louis XI. After the feasts came the time of religious wars. The castle suffered from these times ; king Henry III had the towers levelled in 1585, and so they remained, soberly streaked with white stone. The tapestry has also faded, but now restored, it still provokes admiration. The Angers castle still remains a fine sight.

cing acid, firm-flavoured wines, that are surprising in both their dry and syrupy varieties. Indeed, nowhere else is such a characteristic vine to be found.

Behind the tall walls of the small vineyard of Savennières, these vines produce very distinguished, firm wines, whose dryness demands ten years of maturing before they fully disclose their opulence and persistence. Curnonsky, the "prince of all gastronomes", ranked the Coulée de Serrant among the first five dry white wines of France. This miniature vineyard is now cultivated bio-dynamically: the vines "suffer", so that they yield a very concentrated wine, which is born full and aromatic, then shrouds itself in bitterness for many years before revealing its flavour again.

All around, Savennières-La Roche aux Moines and Savennières are two appellations for wines of the same type, which are allowed, in sunny years, to offer the elegance of a little residual sugar. These wines of great character are the perfect companions for the Loire's pike and zander.

To the south of the Loire lies the territory of the medium-dry and sweet wines of the Coteaux de l'Aubance and Coteaux du Layon domains. Here, the river is the complement of the hillside: the mist that rises from it makes, in good years, "noble rot" develop on the grapes; this microfungus concentrates the juice from the grapes and increases their contents in

The château of Montgeoffroy

Built and furnished in one single effort from 1772 to 1776 by the Marshal of Contades, Montgeoffroy has retained a rare degree of unity. The furniture in its walls is the original one. The dining room, which was an innovation at the time, still features the earthenware stove that the marshal brought back from the town of Strasbourg, of which he was the governor. This is the residence of an elderly soldier, thought out in each of its details, up to the sumptuous kitchen ; the Strasbourg pâté of Foie Gras, that was created for him, is still served here once a year. The copper kitchen utensils are intact to this day. Nothing, not even the French Revolution, could trouble the serenity of the marshal, who died at his lady-friend's home at the age of 92.

sugar. Other vintages yield medium-sweet wines, balanced in sweetness and acidity, that mature marvellously.

Bonnezeaux and Quart-de-Chaume are the two great vintages of this very old vineyard. Wine growers gather every year in Saint-Aubin-de-Luigné for the traditional vintage wine and eel Fair. On this occasion, a few venerable flasks of very old vintages leave their cellars.

But Anjou is also the land of red wines, essentially made from Cabernet-Franc and a little Cabernet-Sauvignon vines. The first variety, that is here nicknamed the "Breton", produces fairly strong

11

The château of Boumois

The château of Boumois is protected by moats. The former outhouses were carried away by floods in the 17th century, as were the remains of the ancient primitive castle. The present-day construction is a fine example of 16th century architecture, covered with tall slated roofs. The Renaissance door still bears a beautiful, finely carved lock.

wines, especially in the area around Brissac. Often matured in barrels, these wines age well for ten years or so, and provide worthy accompaniment to "rillons", which are the local speciality: pieces of bacon are pickled in brine, then browned in lard, and then left to simmer. Finally, caramel is added, which gives them their colour and crispness.

In the cellar of an Angevin wine grower, it is not infrequent to sample no less than ten different wines: a little white wine to awaken taste buds, dry and sweet rosé wines, red wines from various vintages, then syrupy wines, finishing with the "noble grape selections", selections of overripe grapes in which sugar dominates alcohol.

Fabulous cellars can be found here, in which some bottles of the greatest years

The château of Saumur

It is an emblem of the Loire valley ; represented as it was in the "Rich Hours of the Duke of Berry" in the 15th century, it fused the solidity of Middle-Age constructions - a high position and a defensive arsenal - with the splendour of the court of Anjou. History was not kind to it : after becoming a protestant stronghold, the château was then used as a prison for two centuries. The town of Saumur acquired it and saw to its upkeep. Nowadays, it gathers beautiful collections of enamels, sculptures and porcelains, as well as a museum dedicated to horses. It is indeed around the Cadre Noir de Saumur that the French national school of

Ph. A. Laurioux

horse-riding was constituted in 1972. The purpose of this establishment, that is supervised by the Ministry of Sports, is to train professional horse-riders. The Cadre Noir is the school's teaching staff, and perpetuates horse training and dressage traditions. The demonstrations and training the Cadre Noir delivers represent its equestrian conceptions in foreign countries, and strengthen the prestige of French horse-riding.

Ph. A. Laurioux

still lie in their slumber: 1947, 1943 (underrated), 1921, and 1893 which was so fine... Beneath a house in Doué-la-Fontaine, I saw one of these cellars, so damp that no bottles could be labelled, and so deep that old wines had to be removed from it and laid to rest for one year in a medium-deep cellar so that they would consent to ageing a little before being sampled; so that the Layons would take to a little gold for the eye, and the rosés, to a little pink in the cheeks.

This is after all only normal in a town whose rose-garden is renowned for its countless scents. In Doué once again, the Touchais cellar is truly a museum of Coteaux du Layon: millions of bottles are resting here, some over a hundred years old!

Doué-la-Fontaine also possesses many troglodytic houses. Their specificity is that they are not dug into hill flanks as is usually the case, but are in fact positioned

Reconstitution of a troglodytic house in Doué-la-Fontaine.

La Grande Vignolle

Here is an extraordinary château, which rises from the stone on which it has fed : this beautiful tufa, so easy to sculpt, that is extracted from the cliffs on the Loire banks. Who knows where the network of galleries spreading beneath the Champigny vineyard ends ? Nowadays, la Grande Vignolle has become a restaurant.

at the far ends of yards. As a consequence, hardly any sun ever gets into these houses. The subterranean galleries of Dénézé-sous-Doué conceal a genuine treasure: sculpted figurines dated from the 16th century.

In Doué also, one finds a museum of ancient shops: the grocery of yesteryear, with its tin cans and overloaded shelves, always awakens a feeling of nostalgia.

The Loire banks give the opportunity to taste these wines, in restaurants richly decorated with flowers, with an accompaniment of fried fish, salmon, and the renowned pike with Beurre blanc sauce (prepared with shallots reduced in vinegar).

The troglodytic workshop of Richard Rack.

One day when I had, in a prestigious restaurant at Les Rosiers, had some delicious eel stewed in wine sauce for lunch (the eel was swimming in the finest Champigny wine), the owner of the restaurant offered me a little pot of this shallot reduction, cooked for no less than two days on a corner of the stove. A small spoonful was enough to make the sauce reveal all its flavour... if one had the pike! For lack of pike, one shall choose, if it can be found, a shad: this large fish, which travels upstream to lay its eggs, has a very fine flesh. Its only drawback: it has a lot of bones. The alibi of the traditional cooking method, with sorrel, is that it dissolves its bones, the real reason being that it balances its slightly fatty flesh.

Salmon was fished in excessive quantities. The Loire will indeed remain "the last river of Europe", as long as no dam is built on it. But the excessive demand for salmon almost caused it to disappear. It is now only fished according to very strict quotas. Of course, the mere ton of salmon fished every year in the Loire cannot claim to supply all the restaurants.

When it comes to meat, the Anjou offers fine veal, beef cattle of a Le Mans breed, and pork meat specialities: rillons of course, but also andouillette *(Translator's note: small sausage made of chitterlings, that is eaten hot)* and ox tongue.

The mild Angevin cooking is wary of excesses, and never omits a large spoonful of cream to round the flavour of

dishes off. Except in Beurre blanc sauce of course, for it would no longer truly be a Beurre blanc sauce!

In Coutures, the painter Richard Rack has set his art gallery up in a troglodytic manor. The tufa meanders have become the galleries of an original work of art, that is also exhibited in the tropics.

To the north of the Loire, before one reaches the forests, lies the land of the

The castle of Montreuil-Bellay

A fortress said to be impregnable owing to its situation atop a rocky hill, Montreuil-Bellay was reconstructed many a time. Since the construction of the year one thousand stronghold, centuries have raised several walls, an old castle as well as a new one, strange abodes huddled together in the courtyard... But the courtyard, with its wide opening, gives the impression of a nice village hiding behind the walls and posterns that guarded its entrance. The castle's kitchen has also preserved, over the past six hundred years, successive testimonies of the art of cooking.

The famous vineyard of Saumur-Champigny.

Opposite:
**A twisted church tower in
Fontaine-Guérin.**

"boule de fort", also the land of twisted church towers. A European association groups the parishes that possess these strange twisted church towers. This region is rich in beautiful churches, of which Cunault and Candé-Saint-Martin are the finest examples.

Here we are now in Saumur. More than just a stereotyped image of traditional French scenery, the town and its very pure château are a beautiful picture of the Loire. A town constructed over the river, which stretches out between the bridges, Saumur is the city of horses, owing to the Cadre Noir which perpetuates the tradition of equestrian parades in the French army. Every year, officers present dressage shows and harnessing demonstrations.

Saumur is also the town of sparkling wines, the seat of great houses specialised in transformation according to the "champagne method" (even if this term is no longer used out of consideration for champagne wine, the method is still in practise). Saumur wine is no poor man's champagne, but a different sparkling wine, which preserves the acidity and freshness of the Chenin vine.

The Saumur vineyards fluctuate according to trends: white in their majority in the past, they have been replanted with red grape vine to meet the increasing demand for fresh Saumur-Champigny wine, that is pleasant to drink with a midday meal in a restaurant... whereas Champigny is in reality a wine that benefits from being laid to rest, which it always proves, when the vines yield very concentrated juice, that is then granted a little time to mature in casks.

The château of Montsoreau

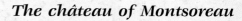

This 15th century fortress stands unfinished on the Loire banks, from which it is now separated by a road. Originally a surveillance château, it is nonetheless adorned with beautiful windows and dormers. The inner courtyard features a fine sample of architecture, the stair tower, which was added to it under François I. Dumas chose this château to be the scene of a famous novel : Charles de Chambres, the betrayed husband, had his rival murdered here. Even if the action in fact took place at the château du Breil in Foin, ten miles to the north, it fits Montsoreau, both harsh and refined, very well indeed.
*The château now offers additional exoticism :
a museum dedicated to the Goums, cavalry units from Northern Africa, the contents of which was brought back from Morocco in 1956.*

Over the past few years, Chenin vines have been planted again, yielding grapes of pleasant mildness, that sometimes produce very syrupy, full wines: the Coteaux de Saumur. One should not forget to pay a visit to Père Cristal's vineyard, in which the vines had been planted in rows against walls: each vine grows across the wall to enjoy the most of the sunshine. The quality of his wines had won this wine grower the friendship of great wine amateurs, and even of the king of England. His vineyard now belongs to the Saumur hospital, but Père Cristal has taken his wine grower's secrets away with him.

The Saumur vineyards grow on a genuine treasure: a thick layer of tufa, this stone so white and tender, with which this region's houses and cathedrals are built. The hills, right through which tunnels have been dug, give shelter to mushrooms, casks, sometimes even families. In Turquant, they shelter apples. Apples "tapped" according to an ancient tradition. Dried, then "tapped" to extract the air from them, candied and dry, they keep for a long time... and will grow young and tasty again when soaked in sauce to accompany roast or poultry.

As it leaves Saumur, the Loire is still quiet, flanked by dikes, lined with roads and restaurants whose only name forces one to stop by: "L'anguille paresseuse", *(The lazy eel)*, how can one resist?

The southern bank rises near the tufa hillsides. Beneath these lie mushroom beds and cellars, some of which are so vast that tractors are brought down into them. Sometimes, an isolated chimney indicates a deep room in which, in summer, one can feast on meat grilled over vine shoots. There is life in the hillsides: only carved façades are visible, the rest lies hidden beneath. Along roadsides, gates are the only hint at the eternally cool galleries that lie behind. It is said that great Bordeaux vintages lie there, left to mature in time by the owners of châteaux in Gironde... but not a word!

In Montsoreau, one celebrates the memory of Balzac's "Dame of Montsoreau", before going to visit the Mushroom museum.

The royal abbey of Fontevraud

The royal abbey of Fontevraud is Europe's largest monastic city. It was founded in 1101 by Robert d'Arbrissel. It was split into several priories, placed under the authority of an abbess, who also commanded the priests. Of the thirty-six abbesses who commanded the order of Fontevraud, half were of royal blood.
The Romanesque kitchens are a spectacular sight, with their stone roofs spiked with pinnacles and twenty-one chimneys. The abbey-church is the Plantagenêt family's necropolis. Henry II, Eleanor of Aquitaine, Richard Lionheart were buried there.
Seized during the French Revolution, turned into a prison in the 19th century, Fontevraud now houses the Centre Culturel de l'Ouest (Arts Centre of the West) and has done for the last twenty years.

Travelling up the Loir valley

Our second stop is sometimes rather unknown. It is nevertheless a charming valley, with many beautiful monuments and a very venerable vineyard. To discover it, one must, near Angers, resist the attraction of the vast, quiet river, and travel upstream along the Loir. The Loir is more than a small sleepy river: indeed, its meanders reach as far as the shadow of the cathedral of Chartres.

This green valley is strewn with beautiful châteaux and water mills with varied productions: at La Flèche, the water mill of La Bruère produces flour, and rather more unusual, refreshing ice. In Vaas, the water mill of Le Rotrou has been turned into a "from flour to bread" museum. In Poncé-sur-le-Loir, the Paillard water mills used to produce paper. They are now a major arts and crafts centre: one can see glassblowers, potters and blacksmiths at work, who not only sell their production, but also transmit their knowledge.

A chemist's jar made in the art earthenware factory of Malicorne.

Haphazardly travelling along the Loir, one will discover other activities, as ancient as they are intriguing: craftsmen making coats of arms, bronze foundries, cabinetmakers, painted furniture makers, trompe-l'œil, cooper's wares, toys, canework, all these ancient crafts are preserved here. At Les Rairies, in the last century, one thousand inhabitants lived off brick-making. All that remains now is three companies and a museum-house. Malicorne, a bit further away, is famous for its artistic earthenware.

One may call the "boule de fort" an "art game" *(Translator's note: "Boules", as well as "Pétanque", are popular French games, quite similar to bowls)*. This game, typical of the Loire valley and of Upper Anjou, reminiscent of both curling and pétanque, is played in large rooms.

The Loir valley also counts a significant number of troglodytic habitations. The municipal cellar of Vouvray-sur-Loir contains a large stone wine press and a baker's oven; every month, it welcomes a market for country produce.

In Marçon, the subterranean cellars are protected by beautiful doors. It is true that we are now drawing near to the jewel of the

Cellar door in Marçon.

Sarthe department, from which most vines disappeared in the last century: the Jasnières. A mythical vineyard of white Chenin wines, that lived through many ups and downs.

The château of Le Plessis-Bourré

Constructed between 1468 and 1473 by Jean Bourré, treasurer to the court of Louis XI, Le Plessis-Bourré is built to face eternity. Its moats are among the widest in France. Scarcely altered, still inhabited, it still retains, in the guardroom, an extraordinary painted ceiling. The patterns, some five centuries later, are still an unsolved mystery. Irony, morality, or alchemy? Located a slight distance away from main tourist roads, Le Plessis-Bourré is nonetheless worth the journey.

Nowadays, the vineyard is very healthy. Jasnières is not an easy wine: highly acid (6 grams per litre is not infrequent, but is actually rather frequent), it retains the most pronounced personality streaks of Chenin Blanc wines whilst parsimoniously rendering their sweetness. Jasnières is in turn dry, medium-dry or even sweet in great years. It is a great wine: firm in the mouth, it develops fine aromas of acacia, of flowers, of quince, of honey. It can mature over long years and,

The château of Durtal

A large mansion overlooking the Loir, Durtal can be read like a panorama depicting the evolution of architecture, from the Middle Ages to the birth of

classicism. Firmly set atop a promontory over the Loir, it watches over the small town. Henry II, Charles IX, Catherine de Médicis and Louis XIII called in at this château.

The "boule de fort"

The situation is delicate to say the least. The opponents are closest to the "petit" (which is equivalent to the jack, for classic bowls players). Dédé takes a run-up, and gently lays his bowl down on the smooth ground. It rolls away, swaying gently, so gently that all think it will never reach its goal. But Dédé pushes it, caresses it with his eyes... then tries to slow it down when it rolls beyond — oh, only a few inches beyond! — the favourable

position. Are they annoying, these flat-shaped bowls, that an off-center weight always throws off balance, seemingly haphazardly.

A few turns later, the whole game is measured and commented while the players "lay a girl" — no harm meant here, this is only a half-bottle of Grolleau rosé, little alcohol and a lot of freshness. Only one opposing bowl stands in the way of Dédé's team. So, standing fast in his carpet slippers, Dédé throws his bowl hard and obliquely. Whereas it hesitated earlier on today, it takes a perfect slanting course, rolls up the raised edges of the pitch, and hits the opposing bowl with force and precision. A perfect "carreau"! (Translator's note: a direct hit on the bowl nearest to the jack) Now, that's how the "boule de fort" is played!

The château of Bazouges

Set between its formal gardens and the Loir, the château is well hidden amidst its grounds. This vast 15th century fortress became, over the centuries, a pleasant residence, whilst still retaining its towers and machicolations, and its seigniorial chapel and windmill.

Troglodytic wine cellar in Jasnières

at its best, will provide perfect accompaniment to the tasty fishes of the Loire and the finest sauces. Good vintages produce full-flavoured dry or sweet wines, that are best kept in a cellar for many years. The hillside is narrow and very long, and is well exposed to the sun.

The Coteaux du Loir vineyards can produce white wines of the same type as the Jasnières. But one will also find light and fruity red wines, as well as rosés. These are often made from Pineau d'Aunis grapes, which give them their characteristic peppery taste, a welcome accompaniment to pork meat specialities. The

The château of Le Lude

This château on the banks of the Loir is well and truly a typical château of the Loire: the Renaissance era pierced the imposing round gothic towers with windows and dormers inspired by Italian architecture. Then, the inner courtyard was adorned in the late Renaissance style, with marble pilasters, pediments and recesses. The Louis XVI façade, constructed in 1787, joined the two main buildings that were once connected by galleries. Classical, of reasonable size, it is a charming sight: as one walks around the château of Le Lude, one discovers several châteaux. The inside of the château is varied too, featuring luxurious vaulted kitchens, brilliantly furnished rooms and a very vast gallery that was remodelled in the 19th century. There is even a small oratory that long remained concealed, and is adorned with 15th century paintings.

What else? Beautiful grounds, and gardens that are looked after and improved with great care. And weekends for gardeners and cooks, when the kitchen is full of the smell of cooking jam...

inhabitants of the Sarthe are, and by far, the world's greatest rillettes eaters. Beyond these vineyards, the Coteaux du Vendômois are rising again in the three colours, in particular with pleasant, unpretentious rosé wines.

Wine grower's chapel in the region of Marçon.

In Lhomme, just around the corner from the vineyard, the Vine museum tells about traditional cultivating methods.

Back onto the left riverbank to admire the old church of Artins, whose foundations are dated from the 3rd century, making it one of the most ancient churches in France.

And back onto the right riverbank, in Trôo, an old medieval town suspended above the Loir. The town grew confined within the little space available between its medieval walls. It is said about Trôo that up to nine levels of cellars are layered beneath the town. The collegiate church of Saint-Martin is a fine example of the Angevin gothic style, dated from the end of the 13th century. The war memorial came here from Bourdelles, but without a statue! Wandering through the streets, one finds a very beautiful well, covered with slates... and it talks! Its forty-five metre depth grants it a faithful echo.

The talking well (45 metres deep) in Trôo.

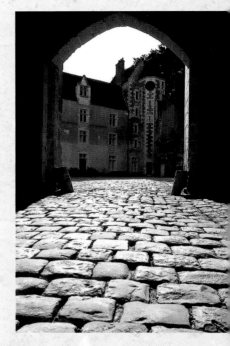

The castle of Courtanvaux

There are some rivers hidden in the countryside that one cannot help but following back to their source. Upstream from the Loir one finds the Braye, and upstream from the Braye one finds the Anille, which leads us to the enormous castle of Courtanvaux. Here, the Renaissance remains austere, and the draw-bridge looks as though it st ready to seal the entrance to the castle!

The château of Poncé

The arbour maze dates back to the 16th century. So does the château, built with white tufa, comprising two buildings surrounding a central pavilion, which holds a superb staircase with sculpted cassoons. Around the château are found gardens, terraces, troglodytic glasshouses and the dovecote with its 8000 pigeon niches, one of the largest in France.
Beneath decorative arcades, the château's outhouses shelter a ethnographic museum dedicated to rural life in the Sarthe.

Trôo also offers a limestone cave, a universe of stalactites and concretions, in which one can see the mineral world at work.

The château of Bois-Freslon, in Ternay, is a beautiful medieval fortress that was renovated during the Renaissance. A stone's throw away, the château of Ranay is a classical château, built of stone and brick, that was raised in the 18th century.

The gothic collegiate church
of Saint-Martin in Trôo.

The ruins of the castle of Montoire-sur-le Loir.

Another keep too stands proud, despite the ravages of time, namely that of Lavardin, which is renowned to be one of the most beautiful villages in France. The remains of this castle rise in tiers on a hillside, and overlook the river from a great height.

The manor of La Possonnière

This beautiful residence is famous owing to the poet Ronsard. A man at arms whose destiny was thwarted by deafness, learned but nonetheless gentlemanly, a poet both lyrical and gallant, Pierre de Ronsard grew up in the family château, that was built at the end of the 14th century. His father, returning home from Italy, had adorned it with sculptures that were the beginnings of the Italian Renaissance; with philosophical maxims too, on the mullioned windows and the beautiful dormers on the roof. The manor of La Possonnière remains intact, as have Ronsard's verses, the testimony of an innovative era.

Opposite:
In the botanical gardens of Roc-en-Tuf in Ternay.

A small distance away, one can visit the Botanical gardens of La Fosse, that feature millions of trees and bushes from around the world. The Loir valley climate suits them well: another park, in Roc-en-Tuf near the town of Montoire, has opened to the public. And another yet in Sasnières, which is very rich in aquatic plants.

Montoire-sur-le-Loir prides itself on the chapel of Saint-Gilles, whose prior was the famous poet Ronsard, who was born in Coutures. The feudal castle now lies in ruins, but the large keep still stands.

In Mazangé, the manor of La Bonna-venture owes its name to an old chapel dedicated to Saint Bonaventure. Renais-sance and Middle Age styles blend toge-ther in charming harmony, hidden behind turreted walls. This château long belonged to the family of the poet Alfred de Vigny.

The château of Rochambeau, built by marshal de Rochambeau, is a rather cold classical edifice, but its chapel is dug into the tufa rock, which is found everywhere in this area. This leads us to Thoré-la-Rochette, a nice village located in the domains of the Coteaux du Vendômois appellation, where the "Maison du vin" (House of Wines) offers introductory courses to wine-tasting. It is installed inside the train station, which is the point of departure of the old railcar, which rejoins Trôo at a snail's pace. And which incidentally travels alongside the track on which the TGV (Translator's note: the

The old village of Lavardin is one amongst the most beautiful in France.

The castle of Lavardin

The cleaved keep of Lavardin still is a fine sight, overlooking its village and the Loir valley from a great height. A triple wall, the gate house, then the ascension towards the keep had made it, since the 11th century, a defensive construction of exceptional strength, that even withstood the assaults led by Richard Lionheart. But the religious wars finally vanquished the mighty edifice: Henry IV had it demolished to punish the Bourbon-Vendôme dynasties. The ruins that remain are nonetheless impressive. In the last century, Viollet-le-Duc considered raising them again... but it was Pierrefonds that was finally chosen. What a shame for Lavardin!

The château of Le Fresne

For nine generations now, the same family has been living in the château of Le Fresne. A classical residence true to form, built in 1765, with a layout that extends into formal gardens and grounds planted with many trees.

French high-speed train) one day reached speeds over 500 kilometres per hour, beating the world record for speed. The railcar also passes through the Montoire train station, where Hitler met marshal Pétain — this was on 24th October 1940 —, and the photo of this sad meeting has since then gone around the world.

Who can ever tell what hides behind the flat façades of the hill of Saint-André? On the road to Villiers-sur-Loire, in Montoire, a narrow road climbs up the steep hillside and leads past these small houses that, like icebergs, only show their tips. Four layers of galleries, mushroom beds and quarries have been dug into the hills. The quarries are now closed, but the mushroom beds are open to visitors.

Our upstream journey along the Loir comes to an end in Vendôme. The TGV has brought this town closer to Paris,

Oyster mushrooms, mushroom beds of Val-Saint-André.

without making it lose its provincial charm. Part of the town was destroyed during the second world war, but nice districts still remain. The Trinity Abbey was founded in the 11th century by the count of Vendôme, and was destined to shelter a

The château of La Mézière

*At a bend in the Loir valley, a small château as there are so many of them, in which one would like to stay for a holiday...
or on a honeymoon, as the parents of Henry IV did at La Mézière. The fine sculpted porch, the Renaissance gallery and the
chimney structures embedded with slates, similar to Chambord, make this château a charming stop.*

replica of the 'Holy Tear', that was brought back from Constantinople. The Romanesque church tower rises to a height of eighty metres, and the church was completed in a flamboyant gothic style, and adorned with a magnificent façade.

Our guiding Loir has in turn spread out in its valley, then been tightly lead between high hills, and here it dawdles along, splitting into several branches which one can travel along in a rowing boat. It still turns the wheels of a few water mills, runs at the feet of a two-hundred year old plane tree, and finally leaves us as it heads towards Chartres. But this is another story.

Opposite:
Panoramic view over Vendôme.

29

The château of Ussé

To the north of the Chinon vineyard, Ussé is a castle that has been turned into a vast, pleasant residence; a composite construction, whose courtyard was opened to the outside when a wing of the castle walls was demolished in the 17th century. It owes its charm to the very different viewpoints it offers, that are all magic in their own way. Do traditions not say that this is "the castle of the Sleeping Beauty"? Indeed, Charles Perrault lived nearby, and came many a time to dream before the castle's towers and keeps.

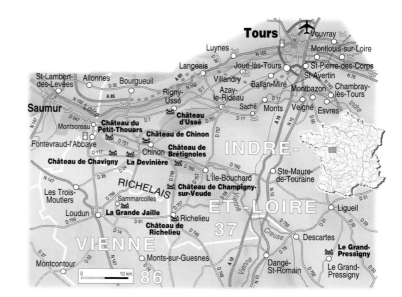

In the homeland of Rabelais, from Chinon to Richelieu

As we travel upstream along the river Vienne, we shall discover a region which was once the scene of bloody wars, epic fights, and merciless battles. But these wars, which are known as "picrocholine", are only imaginary, and indeed born of the wild imagination of François Rabelais, the great man of this region.

Chinon is a small sheltered town, that extends between the banks of the Vienne and the grandiose remains of its historical castle. It is a pleasant and instructive walk through the old streets, that gives visitors the opportunity to enjoy the activities offered by the town: in the beautiful house of the Sates General, where the future king Charles VII raised, in 1428, an army strong enough to fight the English troops, now has settled the Museum of ancient Chinon and of River and canal craft.

Chinon, on the riverbanks of the Vienne.

The chapel of Sainte-Radegonde was dug into the rock in the 11th and 12th centuries. The museum of Wine and Cooperage is an educational place; children will love the automatons, but only grown-ups will be treated to the wine-tasting session.

In the "painted cellars", in which the frescoes have unfortunately faded, is where many chapters in the life of the brotherhood of Rabelaisian "Intoners" took place; they were the lovers of good food and wine, and lived by their credo: "Let us always drink, and never die!"

It is very likely in Chinon that wine jam was invented. Only a Rabelaisian mind could ever capture the aromas of Sauvignon, Chinon or Vouvray wines in sugar. The recipe is simple, but no-one shall disclose its "secrets": heat the wine until it boils, flambé it to burn all the alcohol, add sugar and gelling agents, cook the mixture in a copper pan, and pour it into pots.

White or rosé wine jams can be eaten for breakfast or in yoghurts, whereas red

The castle of Chinon

This is a high place of French history: the Angevin king and king of England Henry II Plantagenêt, who often resided here and raised the fort of Saint-Georges, died here in the year 1189. The castle was already one thousand years old! His heirs Richard Lionheart and Jean sans Terre reigned in its walls until the year 1204, when the castle was taken after a year-long siege. Unceasing wars placed the regions of Anjou and Touraine in the hands of one crown, then of another. In 1214, the Chinon truce returned these territories to the king of France Philippe Auguste, who had the tower of Le Coudray built.

It is in Chinon, in the only just finished royal abode, that Charles VII welcomed Joan of Arc, who had come to support him in his conquest of the French kingdom.

The following centuries witnessed the downfall of this imposing ensemble. Rescued by Prosper Mérimée in the 19th century, the castle of Chinon, whose bell chimes have punctuated the town's existence for the past six hundred years, is nowadays partly restored. The length of its ramparts and the massive shape of its remaining buildings still make it an impressive sight.

wine jam is best served with game, pancakes, or used to thicken meat sauces.

To enter the best red vineyard of the Loire, just walk around the castle. Imbedded in the town, the Clos de l'Echo vineyard (which is said to have belonged to Rabelais' family) stands its aged Cabernet vine stocks in rows against the sloping hillside. Chinon is the homeland of Cabernet-Franc vine, which, when ripe, produces a ruby-red wine, with a fine taste of crushed strawberries, sharp to say the least, and which keeps very well. The vineyard stretches out over the hillsides surrounding the Vienne. Its success also drove it to invade lower and less favourable grounds. One can visit the cellars in Cravant on the right riverbank, and in Sazilly on the left bank, where one also finds the Joguet domain, which still prides itself of a few non-grafted vines.

White Chinon wine is a rarity, made from Chenin vine, which is definitely worth one's attention.

The vineyard at the foot of the castle of Chinon.

The château of Le Petit-Thouars

At the gates of the Touraine vineyards, this château, whose fine outhouses are dug into the rock, bears the name of a hero of the American Civil War. The château has always belonged to the same family, and rules over a Cabernet-Franc vineyard that produces supple and velvety wine.

The château of Chavigny

This old château, which now lies half in ruins, is impressive in a strange way, overruled as it is by ivy and ravens. A kind of gate house guards its entrance, and its outhouses are very beautiful. This is an unusual sight, located near a charming little village.

The town of Candes-Saint-Martin overlooks the confluence of the Vienne and Loire rivers. This beautiful ancient village, in which Martin, bishop of Tours, died in 397, shelters a collegiate church dated from the 12th and 13th centuries.

Between the two rivers stretches a flat region of willow trees and low houses, with, on the horizon, France's oldest nuclear power plant, that is open to visitors.

Beaumont-en-Véron boasts three châteaux and castles: Coulaines, built around 1460, a

Opposite, top:
A few old bottles of Chinon wine.

Opposite, below:
A small boat on the Vienne, at l'île Bouchard.

Lerné is at the very heart of Rabelaisian history. It is around La Devinière, the house where he was born, that the author of *Gargantua* gradually constructed the theatre where his adventures would be played. In Seully, where he learned Latin and Greek, the ancient abbey offers cultural activities and exhibitions.

rectangular residence with very pure architecture. Razilly, a stronghold where Charles VII and Louis XI stayed but which has suffered from the ravages of time. And Velors, which was built in the 15th century, and is surrounded by moats.

Beyond the château of Ussé, the village of Rivarennes still sustains the small industry of "tapped" pears: the pears are peeled whole, and are then dehydrated for four days in a baker's oven, in which they shrink by 70%. They are then "tapped" with a special flattening tool to remove the air from them, and can then be kept dry or be preserved. They then only need to be left to "swell" before cooking, in some red, rosé or white wine, to finely accompany meat and game.

Across the forest of Chinon, one reaches the beautiful village of Crissay-sur-Manse.

The château, which is half-built and half dug into the rock, lies in ruins; the old town is representative of all the charms of Touraine. Nearby, the collegiate church of Les Roches-Tranchelion still raises the remains of its fine gothic architecture. A beautiful keystone is still suspended... in time.

In L'Ile-Bouchard, the river Vienne spreads its branches, as if to clasp the remains of a castle and a charming little

Left:
"Tapped" pears, the speciality of Rivarennes.

La Devinière

The house where Rabelais was born tells far more than many articles dedicated to this great writer. His "pichrocoline wars" (Translator's note: i.e. "petty wrangling wars") ravaged the region, but fortunately only in his books. Rabelais is the great mean of the Chinonais region, where he is stated in every possible way. But after all, his shoulders are strong enough!

The little train running from Richelieu to Chinon.

The remains of the château of Panzoult are remarkable owing to the presence of its 17th century dovecote: a hexagonal tower, that is crowned by a dome, and whose door still carries coats of arms. To the south, the château of Le Rivau in Léméré, formerly a marquisate, is a beautiful fortified residence, that is currently being restored.

We shall now leave the Vienne and head for the Veude, its affluent. And by what better means than the steam train that runs between Chinon and Richelieu? To rediscover the "tchuf-tchuf" sounds of our childhood and once again breathe the smell of smoke in, whilst travelling at speeds of 30 miles per hour. A stop in Ligré gives the opportunity to taste the

medieval town. Of the Romanesque priory still remain the choir and the fantastic bestiary carved into its capitals.

The château of Champigny-sur-Veude

This was once certainly a very beautiful castle. The property of the Bourbon family, the cousins of the kings, it was destroyed by Richelieu, who was at the time both almighty and rather jealous of having such neighbours living next to the town bearing his name. The very nice outhouses are still standing, and so is its gothic holy chapel, which is renowned for the quality of its stained-glass windows.

The castle of Brétignolles

What a fortress! Located to the south of the Chinon wine appellations, hidden behind a tall stone wall, Brétignolles rises in the middle of its grounds, just the way old châteaux are dreamt. An absolutely uncompromising, impressive façade... but this castle, built in the 15th century, nonetheless has no defensive elements to speak of.

Richelieu

A ghost haunting its grounds, the château of Richelieu disappeared, stone after stone, at the time of the French Revolution. The pride of the cardinal, who had sought to construct an ideal town, did not outlive him. And the inhabitants of Richelieu now grow lettuces in the château's moats. The grounds belong to the university of Paris. The only memory that remains of the Cardinal is his coat of arms, which still clings to one of the grounds 's gates.

Chinon wine and cheeses of Sainte-Maure.

Richelieu is the ghost town in the wake of the homonymous marshal's gold rush. A capital without a kingdom, it only lived from the time of its construction to the time of Richelieu's death in 1642. The town's layout is geometrical to the absolute, perfectly square. The beautiful town houses did not prove to be tempting enough to incite the Court to take to the countryside. And the town now bathes in an atmosphere of languidness and quietness, within walls that are too big. Facing the beautiful classical façade of the church of Saint-Vincent-de-Paul, the great halls welcome the market on Mondays, and the wine, cheese and sausage fair every year in the month of July.

The south of Touraine does offer a few fine specialities: the Sainte-Maure-de-Touraine goat's cheeses have an "appellation contrôlée" *(Translator's note: as with wines,*

a label guaranteeing their origin and quality). They come in the shape of a long cylinder, pierced by a straw in its centre, and are strong in taste.

The region also grows asparagus, and, rather unexpectedly, truffles. In the domain of La Pataudière, a charming little château to the north of Richelieu, truffle fields are being planted again, as is the case in the rest of the region, which indeed now counts 120 hectares of woodland. Every year before Christmas, the truffle market of the Richelais region takes place in the town of Marigny-Marmande. The production of truffles, which is subject to uncertain climatic fac-tors, is very variable: from 40 kilograms per year presently, it should soon rise rapidly.

Our travel along the Vienne ends far further along its banks: in Descartes, the town of the great philosopher who laid the foundations of modern science. An adventurer as well as a thinker, René Descartes died in Sweden in 1650. It is not yet completely established that he actually was born in Descartes — it is said that he was born in one of the town's ditches — but it is on the other hand certain that the skull, which is exhibited in here, is a replica.

Left:
Sainte-Maure-de-Touraine goat's cheese.

Le Grand-Pressigny

The oldest of its towers are dated from the 13th century. The keep collapsed only a few years ago. As to the château, it was built in the 16th century and now shelters a large Museum of Prehistory. The tutorial visit gives visitors the opportunity to understand the evolution of techniques, tools, weapons and cooking equipment.

The château of Villandry

From a fine Renaissance château that had been disfigured by 19th century additions to its architecture, Joachim Carvallo created, in 1906, the casket for a garden that is now famous throughout the world. A vegetable garden both ornamental and useful, an ornamental garden inspired by those of Grenada and a classical formal garden "à la française" all cohabit here, and are jealously cared for by his heirs. There are many viewpoints, from one of the terraces or floors of the château, which shelters many works of art and even the ceiling of a Spanish mosque!

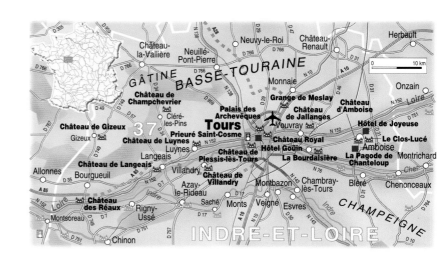

The royal Loire,
from Bourgueil to Amboise

The land extending between the tip of Touraine and the château of Amboise is royal ground indeed. The residences of the Kings of France — Langeais, Plessis-les-Tours, Tours, Amboise — rise amongst the hundreds of known or lesser-known châteaux and castles. Here the Loire is wide and unhurried, it brings water to the "garden of France" and its countless vineyards and vegetable gardens.

The château of Les Réaux

*A stone and brick chequered pattern on the entrance gate house,
streaked patterns alike on the keep, the château of Les Réaux possesses all the
elegance of the first Renaissance era. This is no surprise, since the builders
here are the same as in Chenonceau and Azay-le-Rideau. Can one dream of a
more favourable kinship? The mist rising from the Loire that shrouds it in the
early hours adds to the charm of this inhabited residence, which is open to
passing guests.*

Grapes for Bourgueil wine are picked
in the town of Bourgueil, and those further to the east. One can discern three
"levels" of wines on these grounds:

— "gravel" wines, which are produced
from vines growing at the bottom of the
hillsides and the alluvial terrace overlooking the Loire. They are supple wines,
which do not keep very long, and are
often produced from vines younger than
those on the hillsides;

— wines produced on tufa subsoil.
Strong, concentrated wines that benefit
from being left to age;

— wines from the top of the hillsides,
grown on lighter and sandy soils. These
hillsides are protected from the cold by
the forests of Saint-Nicolas and Benais.

Grapes from older vines are often
converted into wine separately, and
their producers prepare several vintages, from gravel or tufa vines, young

42

or old: there are indeed two distinct, yet intersecting, scales of values, that multiply the expressions of Cabernet-Franc vine. The risk with this type of vine is to produce insufficiently mature wines, that remain sharp in taste with aromas of pepper. Fortunately, the wine production process has evolved considerably.

Generally, the grapes are picked, then left to ferment for a long time, before maturing in large oak casks for a few months, or sometimes more. This is

constantly. These wines are bold and fruity, and finely accompany pork meat specialities and starters.

The Saint-Nicolas-de-Bourgueil "appellation contrôlée" wine is exclusively grown in this town. The vines reach out to the Bourgueil vineyards, and the fairly light soil yields wines that are less tannic and more fruity in taste; but here, once again, the wine grower makes all the difference.

Part of the vineyard used to belong to the Benedictine abbey of Bourgueil,

The vineyard of Saint-Nicolas-de-Bourgueil.

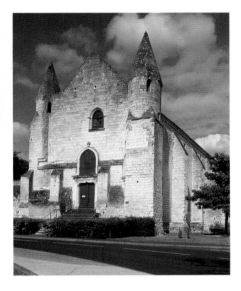

Left:
Abbey of Bourgueil.

when they develop aromas of raspberry and blackcurrant; as a matter of a fact, in the past, the nuns of the abbey would draw the wine through blackcurrant bush branches. This practise has now disappeared, but the wine remembers!

Bourgueil wines also come as rosés, and this production is increasing

The château of Gizeux

Stables, châteaux, galleries, Gizeux stretches out endlessly towards the nearby forest. This fief of the du Bellay family, where two beautiful tombs are concealed in the neighbouring church, has belonged to the same family for the last three centuries.

which has now been turned into a museum. Another museum, in Chouzay-sur-Loire, is dedicated to bargemen: before roads and railways, the Loire river was the quickest and safest means of transport — in spite of the famous constantly moving sandbanks, that require great skill in navigation.

Bourgueil also welcomes fairs: a wine fair of course, at Easter, but also a garlic fair on Sainte-Anne's day, and another fair, dedicated to chestnuts, in October.

The castle of Langeais

The first sight is very austere: at no distance at all, the fortress rises above the village, crowned with machicolations and a rampart walk reaching around it; indeed a stronghold, true to form. The façade overlooking the courtyard is a bit more cheerful, although it is pierced in many places. The ensemble only comprises two of the four wings that had originally been foreseen by Jean Bourré, treasurer to the court of Louis XI, who commanded its construction from 1465 to 1469. In 1491, Langeais was the scene of the marriage of Charles VIII, king of France, with Anne, duchess of Brittany, an event that had considerable repercussions. The interior of the castle has been restored over the last century: magnificent floors, furniture and beautiful tapestries.

Not far out of town, the Moulin Bleu *(Blue Windmill)* has kept its rather unusual colour since the time of the French Revolution. It can rotate on its base to stay in contact with the wind. And, beneath it, lies the inevitable wine cellar.

In Saint-Michel-sur-Loire, the château of Planchoury welcomes a Cadillac museum, dedicated to these huge vessels with a rolling stride, which we all dreamt about someday.

In Lignières-de-Touraine, the manor of Fontenay is a miniature stronghold, defended by battlements and besieged by fruit trees: all the typical sweetness of Touraine.

In Cinq-Mars-la-Pile, near the 13th century castle of the Marquis de Cinq-Mars that inspired Alfred de Vigny, rises a twenty-nine metre tall tower: the proud tombstone of a Gallo-Roman merchant. As to the castle, it was razed to the ground, "to match the infamy" of its master, who was decapitated for organising a plot against Richelieu.

In Savonnières, near the village and château of Villandry, Mother Nature has worked as an artist, first covering the walls of caves, then the steles of men with concretions, which are now true works of

The château of Champchevrier

Surrounded by forests, Champchevrier once was an overnight stop for the kings of France during their hunts. Nowadays, it houses a renowned hunting team and its hounds. The château is comprised of a Renaissance era pavilion and an 18th century construction, which are surrounded by large outhouses. The fine furniture testifies to the fact that the same family has now lived here for the past three centuries.

The manor of Fontenay.

The limestone caves of Savonnières.

The castle of Luynes

The castle of Luynes, belonging to the duke of Luynes, was built in the 12th century on the remains of a former castle. Despite later alterations, it has kept the appearance of a fortress embellished with beautiful gardens. The residence of an important family, it is richly furnished, and its situation overlooking the valley is an added charm.

art. Limestone caves are a journey into a strange world, where time becomes solid and tangible. A prehistoric fauna has also been reconstituted; and as one returns from the bottom of the caves, one can taste a glass of fine, well-earned Touraine wine.

The Touraine vineyards, which are widely spread out and diffuse, are divided into several wine appellations. The generic "Touraine" is especially known for the dry white Sauvignon wines and fresh red Gamay wines. A large part is sold as nouveau wines, as soon as the autumn following the picking of the grapes. Urbanisation has somewhat nibbled at the vineyard of Joué-les-Tours, that Jullien rated in 1866 as producing first-class French wines: "Noble wines, they have a beautiful colour, are full-bodied, have spirit, a very fine taste that is moreover very bold."

The Touraine-Amboise wines use Gamay and Cabernet vines, and a little Cot vine; they remain supple and pleasant; one also finds rosé wines and white wines produced from Chenin vine, which

are dry, medium dry or sweet. The "Commanderie des chevaliers d'Amboise" *(the Chevaliers of Amboise Commander's resi-*

The château of Plessis-les-Tours

Only one wing of King Louis XI's favourite château still stands; here he lived his last years, surrounded by amulets and terrified by his forthcoming death. A great king according to French history, "l'universelle aragne" was also a wily plotter, who first established the principle that promises are only a commitment to those to whom they are made.

dence) takes care of promoting these wines. To the east, the Touraine-Mesland wines are more structured, and produced from the same vines: mainly Gamay, supported by a little Cabernet-Franc and Cot.

Produce of France

CHATEAU DU PETIT THOUARS

CÉPAGE CABERNET FRANC

TOURAINE

APPELLATION TOURAINE CONTROLÉE

MISE EN BOUTEILLE AU CHATEAU

12% VOL   75 cl

COMTE DU PETIT THOUARS, PROPRIÉTAIRE, SAINT-GERMAIN-SUR-VIENNE (I.-&-L.)

the Touraine appellation, the "Noble-Joué" is a very ancient wine, that a small group of wine growers have revived. In the close neighbourhood of Tours, this dry rosé wine, also called a "gris" *(Translator's note: a pale rosé wine),* uses three varieties of pinot vine, and retains the delicious and lost savour of sweets of yesteryear.

But the greatest wine of the Touraine region is the Vouvray. The white Chenin vine produces, over some 1,800 hectares north of the Loire, a wine which can be, according to the wine grower's choice and to the sun's changing moods, dry, medium-dry, sweet or even sparkling. The great vintages of selected grapes, that are overripe or with infested with noble rot, can be

The priory of Saint-Cosme

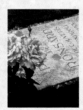

The prior in command of this priory, the gallant Ronsard here wrote some of his finest pages. Beautiful gardens foster roses that, to belie the poet, live longer than just "the space of an instant". Sadly, the church has lain in ruins for a long time now, but it is pleasant to linger here for the place's tranquillity, around Ronsard's tomb, which is decorated with flowers.

Rosé wines, usually dry, and Chenin white wines are also produced here. This small wine appellation, which gathers less than forty wine growers, runs a yearly wine fair. Even though it is only granted

counted to the small society of great syrupy wines. These grapes only grow in the greatest years, such as 1921, 1947 or 1989.

The other vintages yield dry wines, or wines with a hint of residual sugar, which are called "tender wines" in this region.

These wines can accompany all fishes, but also rillettes and goats' cheeses; medium-dry wines are best kept for dessert creams, sweet wines are fine when drunk by themselves, as an accompaniment to foie gras or even (how versatile!) to pleasant desserts with almonds or apples.

Finally, a significant production of sparkling wines fuses the firmness of the Chenin vine with the work according to the "champagne method".

Vouvray wines retain the typical taste of their clay and limestone soil, in which some silica is sometimes also mixed: aromas of ripe or overripe fruit, of apple or quince, of white flowers, or of honey in the case of sweet wines.

The archbishops' palace in Tours

The archiepiscopal palace of Tours, constructed in the 17th and 18th centuries and surrounded by formal gardens, shelters a remarkable museum of Fine Arts. Revolutionary seizures and Napoleon's spoils of war were added to by treasures entrusted to it by the French state. Mantegna, Rubens, Rembrandt, Boucher, Delacroix, Degas, Monet and others… all works of art are featured alongside some luxurious furniture.

The Eco-museum of Vouvray offers a panoramic view over culture and wine-growing. Montlouis, its younger brother from the south of Loire, has the same characteristics, though it is slightly milder. It suffers from a lack of image... and bridges: between the rivers Loire and Cher, this vineyard is isolated on a peninsula, and has an important production of sparkling wines.

Right:
The cathedral of Tours.

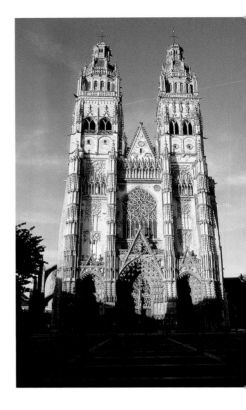

The royal château of Tours

This château once witnessed Louis XI's first marriage, and also his parents': the château of Tours has an illustrious history. Its present days turned out to be more modest: two remaining towers, and a 16th century abode... until the Grévin museum installed a Historical panorama of the Touraine region within its walls. Wax

The city of Tours retains fine memories of its history as the capital of France, at the time when Louis XI, a tireless journeyman, had made it the centre of his administration, thus extending his area of prestige and business. Beautiful town houses, monuments, a cathedral

figurines, dressed with authentic clothes, tell the tales of the great events that were lived on the banks of the Loire, with realism and a sense of detail.

The Goüin town house in Tours

The superb façade, constructed around the year 1500, displays decorations of the Renaissance era, excessively adorned with a loggia and stylistic ornaments inspired by Italian architecture. This fine piece unfortunately burnt down in 1940, during the Loire battle, but has fortunately since then been restored. It now houses the Archaeological museum of Touraine.

which clearly summarises history... Tours lacks no museums: the archiepiscopal palace shelters the museum of Fine Arts, the royal château houses the historical museum of Touraine.

The museum of Saint-Martin reminds us that this bishop was one of the most influential during the first centuries after Christianity was brought to Gaul. His grave lies in a recently-built basilica.

The museum of Trade Guilds contains many masterpieces made by journeying builders. Just beneath, the Touraine Wines museum. Finally, the museum of

51

non-leaded stained glass presents an art as unknown as it is radiant... And in Rochecorbon, on the banks of the Loire, another museum is dedicated to the head-dresses and embroideries of Touraine.

In Rochecorbon also, the manor of Les Basses-Rivières owes its name to the errands of the Loire that flows by at its feet. Built with its back to the cliff, it lends its freshness to a four hundred year-old wine press.

To the south of the Loire, the château of Cangé, raised in the 16th century and flanked with round towers, was partly rebuilt, to a romantic tune, in the 19th century.

In the vineyards of Vouvray, the domain of Valmer conceals a marvellous

The château of Jallanges

Transformed by numerous alterations since the Renaissance era, the château of Jallanges, to the north of the region of Vouvray, is a fine residence of brick and stone, surrounded by vast grounds, also dated from the Renaissance. The family accommodates guests and serves meals. The shop sells forty-seven varieties of home-made jams.

troglodytic chapel, that was dug into the tufa in 1524. The château was built around 1525, and altered afterwards. It does retain an original element, the Petit-Valmer, the very elegant steward's abode. The grounds, which stretch out over several terraces, feature many

Ancient troglodytic habitations in the region of Rochecorbon.

thrust faults and viewpoints. The columns and vases that one discovers here come from the former castle of Chanteloup, in Amboise. And the visit can be concluded with a pleasant tasting session of the domain's wine.

The beautiful troglodytic chapel in the domain of Valmer.

The barn of Meslay

A barn indeed, but what a barn! This outhouse of the abbey of Marmoutiers was raised in 1220. The buildings are very revealing as to what a farm was in the past, both defensive and productive. In an exceptional state of conservation, the barn now welcomes receptions and exhibitions.

La Bourdaisière

If the present appearance of the château of La Bourdaisière is dated from the 19th century, its illustrious memories reach far farther back in time. Indeed, François I and Henry IV gave shelter to their favourites here. Nowadays, one can stay overnight at the château, dreaming of Gabrielle d'Estrées. A large vegetable garden has been created, where ancient varieties of tomatoes are still kept and cultivated. Château of La Bourdaisière, 37270 Montlouis-sur-Loire. Visits from mid-March to mid-November. Phone: 02.47.45.16.31.

A beautiful manor, the château of la Côte lies to the north, in Reugny. A small edifice dated from the Renaissance, it is nicely proportioned, and is adorned with some fine mullioned dormers.

It is said that the pruning of the vines was first thought of in Vouvray... by Saint Martin's own donkey! As it is established that Saint Martin founded the monastery of Marmoutier, in 372, it is likely that the culture of vine followed closely behind him. And the donkey in question necessarily grazed on some grass, so why not on some vine stocks? Saint Martin then realised that the stocks at the edge of the vines — and not at the end of the rows, as is commonly said, for the vines were then "huddled together" and reproduced by layering — yielded grapes that were sweeter in taste and produced better wine. This is how people began pruning vine, which is to date the best way of producing good wine.

In Touraine, one should not forget to taste the rillettes of Tours, which are darker in colour than those of Le Mans. Indeed, while they are cooked, they are treated to a draught of Vouvray wine.

Amboise was the scene of many a king of France's life. Louis XI resided here, and made it a forbidden city to protect his son Charles VIII, who in fact died here after a hard encounter with a door. Anne de Bretagne lived here, and loved this town. François I grew up in Amboise, and called for Leonardo da Vinci. François II, finally, held his court in this town.

The end of the Valois dynasty brought the splendours of the châteaux of the Loire to an end. The towns and stones remain, so does the Loire, Europe's last wild river, and so do the memories of

Amboise

The royal château of Amboise witnessed the birth and death of several kings of France. The buildings that one sees now are only a part of a very large castle that fused late Middle Age and early Renaissance architectures; most of the castle was however destroyed in the last century. With the wealth of its history, brilliantly furnished, Amboise, where lies the body of Leonardo da Vinci, is an illustrious scene of French history.

these times, gathered or recreated.

The "Maison Enchan-tée" *(Enchanted House)* re-enacts this rich history with automatons. And, if hikes are too tiring for you, a "digest" of this history stands at the gates of Amboise: the miniature châteaux theme park, which offers some forty miniature models of châ-teaux of the Loire... to help you feel, for one day, how Gargantua felt. The same company created, in Lussault-sur-Loire, a vast aquarium with many species and attractions. Nearby, the "Fou de l'Ane" *(the "donkey craze")* is a theme park introducing no less than twelve different races of this animal... and a few hybrids. And by the way, a donkey fair takes place every year, on the first Sunday of August, in Savonnières.

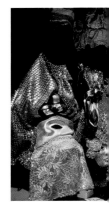

The automatons from the "Enchanted House" in Amboise

Le Clos-Lucé

The manor of Le Clos-Lucé, the residence of Anne de Bretagne, is the residence in which Leonardo da Vinci spent the last years of his life. One can see frescoes that were supervised by the master, and visit his bedroom and other beautiful Renaissance rooms. But this is also a modern place, where models of strange machines, that are often still modern, were built according to Leonardo's sketches, the best proof of his timeless genius.

The pagoda of Chanteloup

The duke of Choiseul, the almighty minister of king Louis XV, was disgraced in 1770, and came to seek refuge in Chanteloup, bringing with him stones from la Bourdaisière. The château was demolished in the 19th century. All that remains of it is this forty-four metre tall pagoda. A Louis XVI style building, inspired by Chinese constructions, this is a unique monument, the greatest "extravagance" from the end of the Ancien Régime.

The Indre valley

If I should give a colour to the valley of the Indre, I would choose green. But a water green, the green of the trees and woods reflecting in the meanders of this affluent of the Loire. And what beautiful châteaux rise around the river!

The château of Azay-le-Rideau is a perfect picture, a graceful monument surrounded by trees and water. Around it lie the village and its vineyard, which, surrounded by orchards, proudly stands its ground.

If the twenty or so wine growers in these surroundings also produce red wines; the Azay-le-Rideau wine appella-

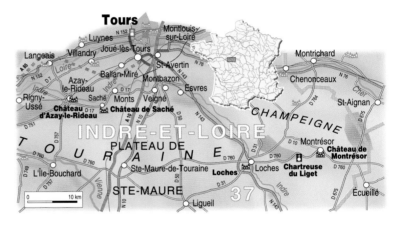

Fisherman's hut on the riverbanks of the Indre.

The château of Azay-le-Rideau

The charm of the château of Azay-le-Rideau would almost make one forget that it once was a defensive fortress. The reconstruction, dated from the 16th century, has made it one of the finest testimonies of the Renaissance and the Italian influence. It contains all their expressions, and of course the magnificent "banister over banister" staircase. Each floor leads to the outside by means of loggias, and the ceilings are adorned with sculpted cassoons. Surrounded by water on three sides, Azay is an architect's dream, and a symbol of the Touraine region's harmony.

tion is exclusively applied to white wines grown from Chenin vines and a few Grolleau rosé wines. These white wines are dry, sometimes medium dry, rarely sweet. They are reminiscent of Vouvray, with more mildness to them.

It is an old windmill that shelters Monsieur Dufresne's museum of Machinery, which he describes as the "most fabulous collection to the glory of modern times"; the construc-

tion also shelters thousands of cars, planes, tractors and even a rolling guillotine!

The town of Cheillé, to the south of the Indre, boasts three châteaux: Chéniers is a 16th century abode near the forest of Chinon, to which a pavilion was added in the century after its construction. La Cour-au-Berruyer, which lies behind a graceful decorated pavilion, is a rectangular-shaped 16th century abode. The château of l'Islette, with its corner turrets and polygonal staircase, is reminiscent of Azay-le-Rideau. It was built in the 16th century on the base of a former building.

A few kilometres south-east of Azay-le-Rideau, in Villaines-les-Rochers, basketry is the traditional way of earning one's living.

"We had travelled to Villaines, where the baskets of this region are made, to order some very beautiful ones indeed…", says a character in *"Lys dans la vallée"* *(Translator's note: "Lys" refers to the French*

The château of Saché

The Renaissance château of Saché, which was partly rebuilt in the 19th century, was a holiday residence for Balzac, who wrote several novels within its walls. Continuously pursued as he was by creditors, he could never treat himself to a château, and often came to stay in Saché. It has since then become the Balzac museum, and houses exhibitions and cultural activities dedicated to him.

Osier plantation in the region of Villaines-les-Rochers, capital of la Valmerie.

royal emblem, the fleur-de-lis), by Balzac, who dropped in many a time, as he lived nearby.

The cooperative provides one third of the French basketry production. Its workshop exhibits all sorts of baskets, eel traps, cradles, bread baskets, chairs, chests large, medium and small, log baskets, and even jugs, whose water-tightness is not guaranteed... And also some flower-holders, cheese or butter dishes, dishes also for sardines, strawberries or salad, a potato riddle, and tables, sofas, a beautiful horn of plenty... let us stop here, you shall see all the rest on the spot! As to the willow plantations, they can be seen from roadsides all around.

After Saché, which became famous thanks to Balzac's frequent stops in town,

Loches

The collegiate church of Saint-Ours rises between the royal abode and the keep. The abode carries fond memories of women: of Joan of Arc, who met "her" king Charles VII, who had completed the construction of the "Logis Vieux" (the "Olde Abode") for Agnès Sorel, his beautiful favourite, who lies here. Anne de Bretagne, whose first husband, Charles VIII, built the Logis Neuf (the New Abode), and whose second husband, Louis XII, raised the fine oratory.
The keep of Loches, built by Foulques Nerra in the 11th century, is rather less pleasant: a massive shape, with few openings, it has lost nothing of its power. Its entrance is placed at a great height above dry moats. An impregnable refuge, surrounded by walls and outhouses that were used as dungeons by the kings of France, then by the new-born Republic.

61

the banks of the Indre dawdle along the roadside. In no particular order, one can see the beautiful water mill of Beaumer, with its cast-iron wheels, little châteaux that inspired many descriptions in Dante's "Human Comedy", and everywhere, small fishermen's huts are perched over the river. On sunny days, this is a fine site for picnicking whilst tackling eels and pikes.

The manor of Vonnes is described in *"Le Lys dans la vallée"*. It is a building surrounded by two pavilions with tall slated roofs. In Montbazon, a large keep still stands, raised by Foulques Nerra and therefore dated from around the year one thousand. The manor of La Belle-Jonchère in Veigné is a far more welcoming sight, with its tall roof and its statuary applied to a 16th century body.

The church tower of Esvres is covered with stone. The church's façade is embellished with Merovingian slabs of stone. The Indre then takes us to Cormery, which is renowned for its macaroons; their invention is in fact the subject of a fight with the Italian town of Venice. Cormery is also famous for its very ancient abbey dedicated to Saint Paul. The cellar, the pond, the joiner's workshop and lock house are scattered throughout the town, which also offers visitors the pleasant sight of beautiful old houses.

A few kilometres further, on the side of the main road, a 20th century "extravagance" has been created: every summer,

The water mill of Beaumer

The Charterhouse of Le Liget

Raised in the 12th century by Henry II Plantagenêt, to apologise for the murder of Thomas Becket (who had excommunicated him), this beautiful monastery stands at the end of a long alley. The splendid gates are dated from the 18th century.

the world's most beautiful cornfield grows in a different light. A gigantic maze in which one can have fun losing oneself in a setting that changes every year. Brought to life by comedians, it is also, at night when the moon is full, a very strange and intriguing site. As Ronsard would have said, it lives "the space of a summer".

The rivers Indre and Indrois then part ways, overlooked by the beautiful manor

The Maze Gardens in Reignac-sur-Indre, a splendid creation with plants, on a different theme every year.

*The town of Loches
seen from the château.*

keep retains memories of the battles and affirmation of the royal authority.

In the royal abodes are kept two paintings by Jehan Fouquet, a painter from Touraine, who lived in the 15th century. A beautiful triptych of the Passion, and a portrait of Agnès Sorel, the courtesan, as the nursing Virgin Mary! A very fine altarpiece by Fouquet, a Pietà in cold colour tones, is also found in the church of Nouans-les-Fontaines, near Montrésor.

Sinister memories of the dungeons in the keep of Loches cannot tarnish the beauty of the old town, which reaches from the base of the solid walls down to the lower city gates. The suburbs extend far beyond the fallen walls, but beautiful old houses can still be seen.

And, as one leaves the town, one finds a troglodytic quarry that stretches out in endless kilometres of galleries. Fossils embedded in the Vignemont quarry's tufa walls are a reminder that this rock was formed beneath the sea, some 90 million years ago. In the middle of this world of silence towers a fountain, facing a mushroom bed, showing that men always make the most of natural curiosities.

The region of Loches is the breeding ground of the "black Dame", which is a breed of hens that was obtained by crossbreeding at the beginning of the century. The name is rather deceptive, as only this Touraine hen's feathers are indeed black: its flesh is very white, as the corn which is used to feed it.

This is where the known and waymarked path comes to an end, and tourists soon head back to the banks of the Loire to discover other prestigious visits. But if one takes the time to stroll along the banks of the Indre, one discovers many more beautiful châteaux and castles.

To the west of Loches, the castle of Grillemont, which rises above La Chapelle-Blanche-Saint-Martin, is a large fortress that was built in the 15th century by the governor of Loches, and fitted out as a residence some two hundred years later.

The château of Verneuil-sur-Indre, the seat of an 18th century marquisate, is a vast classical residence. In Bridoré rises an imposing and austere fortress, defended by a forecourt and ditches, which have now been filled with earth. Caesar's tower, in Châtillon-sur-Indre, has been

of La Follaine. The Indrois leads us to Montrésor, whose very ancient château overlooks a village of steep alleyways.

The Indre takes us to Loches, where the romantic poet Alfred de Vigny was born; but over and above all, Loches is a special page in the book of French history.

The royal abode tells us of Anne de Bretagne and the beautiful Agnès Sorel. The

turned into a water tower! This is, once again, a keep built by Foulques Nerra; the adjoining château was built in the 13th century.

In Clion, on the banks of the Indre,

stained-glass window from the château of Loches.

the castle of l'Isle-Savary is a beautiful gothic construction that dates back to the 15th century, equipped with square corner turrets. The centuries following its construction softened its austere fortress appearance, as its courtyard was opened to the outside.

The château of Palluau-sur-Indre still has a tower that dates back to the 12th century, whose walls are nearly 10 metres thick at their base! The beautiful gothic abode, the one hundred metre deep well, the immense subterranean rooms are some added charms it offers.

The walls of the castle of Le Mée, in Pellevoisin, were pierced with windows in

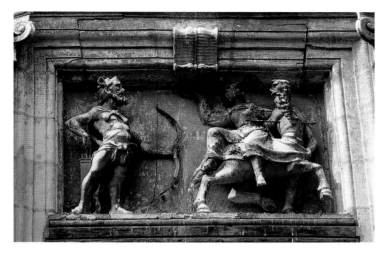

A bas-relief in Loches.

the 17th century. The castle has nonetheless kept a defensive appearance, equipped with four turrets and a subterranean guards room.

The château of Argy, near the town of Buzançais, fuses the defensive architecture of its keep and rampart walk with the opulence of its ornaments, entwined ermines and fleur-de-lis. Its 12th century fortified farm completes this superb rural ensemble.

The castle of Montrésor

The treasure within these walls is that of the kings of Poland, which is kept next to Italian masterpieces in the only remaining wing of the castle of Montrésor. The most ancient buildings here date back to the year 1005! With its two sets of walls and two rampart walks, Montrésor watched over the river Indrois, which is an affluent of the Indre.

The Cher valley

It is near Tours that we shall follow the Cher valley, that runs along the border of Sologne towards the region of Bourges.

Many châteaux and castles are scattered along the riverbanks. Azay-sur-Cher, the ruins of a fortress that was burnt down during the Hundred Years' War; Leugny, a sober classical construction that belonged to the Descartes family.

And the wine-growing château of Nitray, which takes us to the most famous of all, Chenonceau. It can of course be visited on foot, but one can also discover it on board a river boat, or even a hot air balloon.

The fine wines from the domain of Chenonceau, red and white, dry or sometimes sweet, all carry the Touraine wine appellation. It is well-known that Diane de Poitiers, when Chenonceau still belonged to her, took great care of her vineyard.

A few steps away, between Chisseaux and Chissay, stands the opening of the "Fraise Or" distillery, adorned with beautiful retro-style gates. The rest, of course, is buried in the penumbra of the caves.

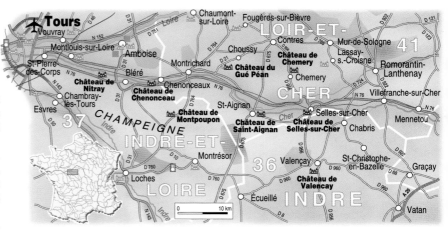

The Chenonceau vineyard

A historical feature since the time of the Renaissance, akin to the famous château anchored in the riverbed of the Cher, the Chenonceau vineyard still honours the memories of the women who cared for the monument and the vine stocks throughout the centuries until today. It was the duty of the Touraine to consecrate this mythical union: Dionysos at Aphrodite's feet!

Regardless of its presence on the finest tables of France, the shipping of the "Château de Chenonceau" to the opposite end of the world has allowed it to acquire a reputation that was consecrated by the most demanding critics and the highest distinctions.

The vineyard's attachment to its château - unless it is the other way round - also enables us to offer our visitors the pleasure of leaving with a very pleasant Bacchic souvenir of the Val de Loire's finest vineyard. BERNARD VOISIN CURATOR OF THE CHÂTEAU OF CHENONCEAU

The château of Nitray

The "Gazette de Nitray" (Translator's note: the local newspaper) *regularly carries news about this château, which is also a wine-growing domain of the Touraine wine appellation. The Renaissance château is surrounded by beautiful outhouses. Here one can have lunch, taste the domain's wines, and visit "la Cité de la Vigne et du Vin" (The city of Vine and Wine)... and even take part in the wine harvest!*

The château of Chenonceau

At this point, the river Cher narrows and shrouds itself in woods as it peacefully runs beneath the arches of the most beautiful bridge-château there can ever be. A women's château: constructed by the Bohier family in the 16th century, it was then confiscated by king Henry II, who offered it to the fair Diane de Poitiers. But, as a rule, favourites don't do too well after the prince's death: at the death of Henry II, Catherine de Médicis reclaimed Chenonceau, offering Chaumont-sur-Loire in exchange, where Diane never went. Diane is to thank for the garden of the riverbank of the Cher, and Catherine for the gallery over the bridge; after the time of celebrations came the time to mourn, when queen Louise, the widow of Henry III, died. Chenonceau was abandoned for a century, then lived prosperous times again thanks to Madame Dupin, the friend of artists and writers.

Reasonable in size, perfected in its slightest details, Chenonceau is indeed a residence fit for a queen.

In Montrichard, one finds a large cellar of Crémant de Loire wines. This young wine appellation has somewhat replaced the sparkling wine of Touraine, with quality standards as high as those of Champagne. But one should not forget to taste the sparkling red Touraine wine, a local curiosity, a treat to accompany some fine ripe strawberries.

The cellars of Monmousseau also house the museum of European Brotherhoods: with their coloured costumes and language, and the merry chapters of their lives, they are the keepers of the taste for good food and wine, and the ambassadors of traditions.

An old keep, built in 1010 by Foulques Nerra, watches over the town of Montrichard. It houses several museums, and now offers demonstrations of birds of prey in flight.

An aviary of birds of prey, the "Keep of the eagles", in Montrichard.

The château of Montpoupon

The old château of Montpoupon has retained a medieval aspect, in spite of the Renaissance additions it features, among which a beautiful pavilion that stands at its entrance. The outhouses now welcome a museum of Huntsmen, which offers a complete panorama of the art of hunting with hounds.

Bourré is arguably the most troglodytic village of all, since half of its inhabitants live in the caves from which was extracted the stone used to build the châteaux of the Loire: there are over 300 km of galleries! The extraction came to an end in 1932,

A cocoonery (silkworm breeding farm) in Bourrée.

Troglodytic mushroom beds in Bourrée.

and gave way to mushroom colonies: cultivated Paris mushrooms of course, but also oyster mushrooms, and then the large wood blewits (or "blue foot"), and now even the Japanese shii-take.

The temperate atmosphere of the caves also suits silkworms, whose breeding has been taken up again, after being abandoned for many years. Louis XI ordered the plantation of the blackberry bushes, which caterpillars are so fond of. The silkworm cocoonery of Bourrée is also a museum of troglodytic life.

The town of Pontlevoy prides itself of its 11th century abbey. It shelters several museums, one of which is dedicated to chocolate: Auguste Poulain was born in

The château of Le Gué-Péan

Surrounded by forests and prairies, the château of Gué-Péan leads, slightly set back from large tourist roads, a quiet existence that began in the 16th century. Various styles combine without clashes around a square courtyard. The interior displays rich 18th century furniture.

*A capital of the church
of Saint-Aignan-sur-Cher.*

Pontlevoy in 1825. An industrialist, he was also a forerunner in terms of advertisement, of which the museum displays many tasty, amusing or instructive examples.

In Thésée-la-Romaine, a 2nd century wall stands near a museum presenting the search results of this large Gallo-Roman centre.

Saint-Aignan-sur-Cher, between its château and the river, has some fine ancient houses and a very pure Romanesque-style collegiate church. With its two square church towers and the bestiary sculpted into its capitals, it is one of the region's finest churches.

We are at the heart of the region of goat cheeses. The goat's cheese of Selles-sur-Cher is renowned, and benefits from an "appellation contrôlée", similarly to wines. It is shaped as a flat disc, that is white and firm inside, beneath a crust coated with wood ash.

The château of Saint-Aignan

The château of Saint-Aignan-sur-Cher overlooks the town from a rocky peak. Surrounded by immense walls, the castle was replaced, in the Renaissance era, by a beautiful building. It can be accessed by a beautiful, wide staircase whose balustrades are gashed by the claws of time.

The château of Chemery

Chemery is a charming little château indeed! An edifice dated from the 15th and 16th centuries, that was then used as a farm, it has been renovated over the last few years. Rising behind its moats, it is a square construction surrounded by constructions and an abode of contrasting feudal and Renaissance styles. The keep is a strange sight: polygonal at its base, it becomes square as it rises.

Thésée-la-Romaine, a 2nd century AD Gallo-Roman site.

The châteaû of Selles-sur Cher

The Middle-Age fortress was razed to the ground by Richa Lionheart. But Philip de Béthune, brother Sully, rebuilt the cas in the 17th century. drawbridge steps ove the moats, which are among the largest in France, and leads to long wall of arcades that connects the two pavilions. The trees the grounds and the Cher riverbank softe the harshness of thes constructions from early times.

Further to the south, Valencay is a cheese shaped like a peculiar truncated pyramid; here is its story: Talleyrand's prince one day offered Napoleon a small cheese from his home-region. The Emperor, to taste it, cut its tip off with his sword. And so this shape was chosen! The Valençay cheese is often also coated with wood ash, and is characteristic owing to its fine taste of hazelnut.

Talleyrand's cook was no less than the great Antonin Carême, the leading chef in the French cooking tradition and an incomparable baker and pastry cook. Facing the château, Jacky Chichery perpetuates this tradition. He even made a Valençay château out of sugar!

The vineyard of Valençay is scattered throughout the woods and fields. The vines are planted in clayey soil containing "blond flint" and tufa chalk. They yield red Gamay wines, but also fine white Sauvignon wines, with a hint of fullness brought by the Chardonnay grapes. Of course, they marry perfectly with the local cheeses. Faverolles, to the west of Valençay, is the birthplace of an old breed of good laying hens, whose flesh is also delectable. Their breeding is now picking up after having nearly disappeared for a while.

The vines of Valencay.

The sugar château of Valencay, made by the pastry chef Jacky Chichery.

Around Valençay, many châteaux rise on the banks of the Cher's affluent rivers: the Modon, the Nahon, the Céphons and the rather unknown Renon.

Luçay-le-Male, a large feudal castle that was partly rebuilt in the Renaissance era, still belonged to the domain of Valençay when it became the property of Talleyrand. The château was then reduced to a farm, before it was recently restored by an attentive owner. Veuil, a beautiful Renaissance residence, suffered the same fate, but did not get the same chance.

The château of La Moustière, in Vicq-sur-Nahon, is a perfect example of classicism: an abode with a triangular pediment, projections and small pavilions on its sides, with beautiful outhouses and a chapel; they form a balanced ensemble, which is moreover constructed on a superb site overlooking the river.

In the castle of Entraigues in Langé, stone masons discovered, in the last century, the skeleton of young woman, richly clothed, who had been walled up

The riverbanks of the Cher.

alive... A dark episode in the life of this large medieval abode, flanked by tall round towers.

Further to the south, the château of Bouges is a twin brother of the Petit Trianon in Versailles. Beautiful furniture, grounds featuring many rare species of trees, horse-drawn cars and a saddlery are all the more reasons to pay this château a visit.

The château of Valençay

Son et lumière shows, plays and acts in authentic clothes, wine-tasting sessions, horse riding and more, the Indre department has made the château of Valençay a truly inevitable rendezvous for tourists. It is true that this superb palace, that was raised in the 16th and 17th centuries, is a marvellous example of the Renaissance style chased by the appearing classicism. Over one hundred luxuriously furnished rooms containing tapestries, and the table on which was signed the Vienna treaty brought back by Talleyrand, the most famous guest to have called in at this residence. The king of diplomats, who outlived all the governments and regimes, was installed in Valençay by Napoleon, in order to welcome the guests of France. From Valençay, he lead the French nation's politics, serving Napoleon then Louis XVIII with the same stunning virtuosity. He now rests near his château.

The château of Chambord

"The base of this strange monument is, as the château, full of elegance and mystery: a double-helix staircase that rises, in two entwined spirals, from the foundations up above the highest church towers, and ends with a lantern or a windowed cabinet, crowned with a colossal fleur-de-lis, that is seen from afar... It is like fleeting thought, a brilliant reverie that would suddenly have earned a durable body; it is a dream made real" (Alfred de Vigny). How can such a large château seem so gracious, so abundant in spirit? Yet another mystery for Chambord. Over four hundred rooms, one chimney for each day of the year, seventy-five staircases, Chambord is a challenge to logic. One thinks one knows it by the plan, which is basically very simple: a central staircase, a layout in the shape of a Greek cross that leads to identical apartments at each floor; and then one loses oneself in small windowless rooms, one suspects mezzanines and hidden staircases. One thinks it to be perfectly symmetrical; and yet each façade bears slight imbalances, galleries added

➤ ➤ ➤ continued p.87

Ph. H. Champollion

The Loire of Blois and Chambord

The region of Blois is one of the Loire regions that counts the largest number of châteaux and castles, both small and large. Five centuries later, one still senses the influence of the Valois dynasty, who in time held their itinerant court here, and built some prestigious châteaux.

Richly covered with forests, the sou-

The château of Chaumont-sur-Loire

Only three buildings remain of the château that was raised, in the late 15th century by Pierre d'Amboise, on the ruins of the previous castle which Louis XI had demolished. This large ensemble, which is half gothic and half Renaissance, once welcomed Catherine de Médicis and her astrologer and secret counsellor Ruggieri; Diane de Poitiers, who usually gave her preference to her residence in Anet; Madame de Staël, banished from Paris by Napoleon; and the princess de Broglie, who adorned it with the splendours of the 1900s and had stables built for her horses, and many other animals too - and even an elephant! Every year, this château welcomes the international garden fair, where one can discover plants and landscapes from all around the world, whilst watching the Loire flow by.

thern bank of the Loire welcomes several châteaux of great interest, such as Chaumont or Beauregard. This land, one part of which lies in the region of the Loire, and its other part in Sologne, collects the waters of the rivers Cosson and Beuvron; these are in fact the waters from Sologne, which flow into the Loire after encircling the town of Candé-sur-Beuvron. This town was once a harbour on the Loire, but alluvial deposits gradually diverted the river away from it.

Near Fougères-sur-Bièvre, the château of Roujoux is a Louis XIII abode, whose tower is crowned by a dome with a pinnacle. Its history is told by automatons, from the time of the Vikings to the 20th century.

From a damp and mosquito-infested area of Sologne, François I raised the most sumptuous hunting meet of all. Chambord,

although it was only rarely inhabited, has deeply altered its surroundings: the Cosson, which is canalised, is now a nice site for a trip in a small boat. But one may also prefer a promenade in a horse-drawn barouche.

The closed-in four thousand square metre grounds are partly accessible to visitors, so one may observe wild animals, and hear stags bell when autumn comes. The château shelters a large Hunting museum, that features works of art by Desportes, Oudry and many others. The June "Game Fair" is the inevitable rendezvous for hunters, gunsmiths and breeders.

Saint-Dyé-sur-Loire, a stop on the way to Saint-Jacques-de-Compostelle, was the harbour where the construction materials used for Chambord were unloaded from

A beautiful walk around Saint-Dié-sur-Loir, the harbour of Chambord.

The castle of Fougères-sur-Bièvre

The castle of Fougères-sur-Bièvre is a square-shaped edifice that is well defended by an old keep and a tall gate house at its entrance, typical of the gothic era. Inside the castle, the change of scenery is complete. With its galleries built over arcades inspired by the château of Blois, the very decorative pediments adorning its doors and the pinnacles at the top of its turrets, the inner courtyard looks like that of a town house. A demonstration in the art of living happily, once the gates are closed.

boats. And also the residence of François I during the construction works, that then became the residence of the château's inhabitants: even royal will could not prevent swarms of mosquitoes from returning every summer! One can also visit the church where lies Dié, also known as Déodat, a hermit who lived in the 6th century.

Nearby, in Saint-Claude-de-Diray, a farm grows... yams! This exotic vegetable, which is the tropical equivalent of potatoes, seems to have adapted itself well here, since a yam fair takes place every year in April in this town.

The vineyards in the Touraine wine appellation reach out as far as Blois. But no wine is produced here any more, and definitely no more "black wine", whose only merit was to strengthen any rather thin red wines; or even, at a ratio of one to six, to change white wine into red wine!

Between Blois and Onzain, the "côte des Grouets" was, in the last century, very well-known for its coloured red wines, that kept very well.

The château of Blois is a résumé of the French Renaissance... and of the periods that followed it. At the other end of the vast entrance place, a large, impressive house conceals countless traps, illusions and enchantments. In the attic, the "academy

A beautiful walk around Saint-Dié-sur-Loir, the harbour of Chambord.

The château of Beauregard

The château of Beauregard is famous for its gallery of portraits of illustrious men and women, that was ordered in the 17th century by Paul Ardier, a former minister under Henry IV. Three hundred and twenty-seven sovereigns, scholars, scientists and writers adorn the walls of the gallery, the floor of which is an army of 5600 Delftware soldiers. A unique piece, sheltered in a gallery constructed in the 17th century at the angle of a fine 16th century abode. The recent Garden of portraits is a country-like extension to this page of History.

The royal château of Blois

The kings of France did grant the château of Blois all their attention for many years; indeed, many held their court here. The 13th century fortress of the counts of Blois received an additional wing and a gallery under Louis XII; another wing under François I, that featured the château's now famous helix staircase, an innovation inspired by Italy; and the "façade des Loges", a grandiose accumulation of loggias facing the town. In the 17th century, Gaston d'Orléans, brother of Louis XIII, built another wing, in a classical style, destroying a building dated from Louis XII in the process. He intended to remodel the entire château, but — fortunately — had to abandon, for lack of means, and stayed in the ancient château, contemplating his unfinished dreams.
This is where, in 1429, Joan of Arc raised her army, and where her standard was blessed before she rode, on the 14th of April, to free the

of secrets" jealously guards tricks which are only ever given by word of mouth from magicians to magicians. For here indeed is the Robert-Houdin museum, dedicated to the "master of all magicians", who was born in Blois in 1805.

Every day, at noon, a six-headed dragon appears at the windows, facing the equestrian statue of Louis XII.

In Blois also, the museum of Objects offers a strange retrospective of contemporary sculpture and art. The museum of

town of Orleans. And where, in 1588, the duke de Guise, who commanded the military during the Saint Bartholomew's day massacre, was assassinated.
The inside of the château, which was in time used as a barracks, was intensively restored in the 19th century. It contains noticeable features such as monumental fireplaces, a model which inspired countless others in France.

Fine Arts is more classical, presenting many beautiful works of art from the Renaissance. Blois is also an enamel production centre. And also the town that gave birth to Denis Papin, the inventor of the steam engine, to whom a statue pays tri-

bute, standing on the staircase that leads from the lower town to the upper town. No hard feelings from Blois, a major French town of stud farms, where one can observe the love rites of stallions of ancient breeds of workhorses, which have long since been replaced by farming machines.

The imposing 19th century grain market has been listed on the historical register, and now shelters a cultural centre. The old

A detail from one of the entrances leading to the Castle of Blois.

The château of Ménars

The château of Ménars, a Louis XIII style edifice, once belonged to Colbert and to the Marquise de Pompadour. Its grounds are superb, but one shall especially remember the gardens that stretch out to the Loire, and that one can admire from the opposite riverbank.

streets tumble down towards the Loire from the Puits-Chatel district, which survived the bombings during the last war.

A string of beautiful residences stretches out along the right riverbank of the Loire, between the road and the river: the château of Saint-Denis-sur-Loire dates from the 17th century. It was built on the remains of a former stronghold. The château of Cour-

sur-Loire was once the property of the marquise de Pompadour. It is raised on a very pleasant site overlooking the river. The 15th century construction was then heavily adorned with turrets. The château of Les Forges, in Suèvres, is connected to the village church via an underground passage. Modest in size, it is nonetheless a genuine seigniorial residence with its flat-sided turret and machicolations.

In the 16th century, the d'Avaray family had one bit of bad luck after another: one of its members almost blinded François I in one eye during some celebrations. Another member, Gabriel de Lorges, jousting in tournament against the aforementioned king's son, king Henry II, broke his lance, which pierced the king's eye. The doctors of the Court tried to save him by all means, and did not even hesitate to decapitate four

The château of Talcy

A rustic 16th century château, with its roofed well, its huge wine press and its dovecote, raised by an Italian banker, whose daughter was the Cassandra that Ronsard celebrated: "Sweetheart, let us see if the rose..."
Diane Salviati, Cassandra's niece, was the impossible love, for religious reasons, and the Muse of the poet Agrippa d'Aubigné.

➤ ➤ ➤

The château of Chambord (page 78 continued)

or obstructed, a staircase too many, not to mention the formidable anarchy that reigns on the rooftops, where a village literally seems to be camping around the chimneys. Chambord is a château that is unique by the political project it represents. In a poor and swampy region, where the only pleasure that could attract the king of France was that of hunting, Chambord was born under favourable auspices: a powerful king, François I, and yielding times, the Renaissance. What part did Leonardo da Vinci play in this project? It is established that at least the staircase is his work. And for the rest, let us only thank the atmosphere that reigned at that time, that the architecture reflects. The defensive fortress fades behind the pleasures of life, of fresh air and celebrations. The large round towers are a speech about power, but a power that is confident in itself: a political power, rather than a garrison on the alert. The Emperor Charles the Fifth was speechless before this edifice, as he cried out: "it is a synthesis of what the human mind can achieve best". He probably also saw a certainty in this château: France had become a great kingdom.

But maybe did the realisation exceed the project. To such an extent, in fact, that the royal apartments had to be built "nearby": the château itself is the crown and needs no sovereign. Each occupant here seems to have been but a tenant, who tried to settle in as he wished during his lease... And Chambord has lived through centuries, so untouched by these transformations that one can imagine it rising unchanged in a few hundred years' time. Still standing in Sologne like a huge diamond in the middle of France. With the casket to match: gardens as vast as Paris, surrounded by the longest wall in Europe.

prisoners to closely study their heads! Nonetheless, the king died ten days later... Finally, the château, surrounded by moats, was partly rebuilt in the 18th century, whilst retaining its ancient towers.

Set slightly away from tourist roads, Talcy is well worth the detour, for its château and beautiful rotating windmill, that is still used to grind flour. Its base is made of stone, and the windmill is made of wood. This kind of windmill was driven by a donkey tied to a long wooden shaft: donkeys do not like wind, probably because of their long ears. They always sought shelter behind the windmill, thus always turning the blades towards the wind.

Top left:
The rotating windmill near Talcy.

The Loire in Blois.

The château of Cheverny

Watching over the entrance of Sologne, the château of Cheverny rises amidst large grounds which highlight the whiteness of the Bourré stone used for its construction. A Louis XIII style edifice, it is perfectly symmetrical, and is furnished with many beautiful tapestries, that are in remarkable state. The grounds shelter an orange grove, and the kennels of the Cheverny hunting team. The trophy room contains no less than 2000 trophies of stags caught by this team.

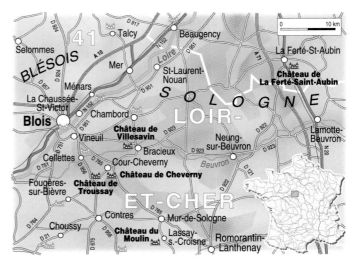

S o l o g n e

Like a sea ruled by tides, the region of Sologne shifts between borders that are given to or taken back from it. Once divided between the county of Bois, the duchy of Orleans and the duchy of Berry, Sologne now is on the border of three French departments. It owes its unity to its landscapes. May we be forgiven for

The château of Villesavin

When François I, who was captured at the battle of Pavie, returned from captivity in 1526, he entrusted the construction site of Chambord to Jean Le Breton, who had shared his fate. Le Breton was very likely inspired by some of the ideas applied here when he built his château in Villesavin, which is only a stone's throw away from Chambord. The result is a charming residence, harmonious and tastefully decorated.

here. Around Cheverny, it has been given the name of the Cour-Cheverny "appellation contrôlée". These white wines have a pale colour, are dry, lively, frankly acid and have a decently long finish. They often present a strange salty note that makes them fine companions for oysters and seafood.

The Cheverny wine appellation is

having torn borders away from it, that were openly connected to other routes. Before we enter the region, let us talk a little about vines.

In 1519, François I ordered 80,000 vine stocks from Bourgogne, to cultivate them around his château in Romorantin. This variety was naturally given the name of Romorantin vine, and has only survived

The château of Troussay

The little manor house of Troussay, built in 1450, is a lovely little château, with an abode adorned with two levels of mullioned windows and two wings ending with turrets. The outhouses are larger in size, which is quite normal for a rural domain. The formal vegetable garden is bordered with old box trees.
Troussay is also a museum of Traditional life in Sologne.

only a century old: Sologne used to be a vast stretch of insalubrious marshes, interspersed with moors, even though the region was fairly rich at the time when the kings of France held their Court here. Sheep farms then neighboured with crops. In Fontaine-en-Sologne, one can visit a large farm that prepares many lamb specialities.

Napoleon III is to thank for a vast draining project: forests were planted, ponds and canals were created. The imperial family owned large domains in Sologne.

Since then, hunting has grown to be of considerable importance; hunts in large domains, with appointed areas, game farms and traps set for rodents. Or the less noble hunting sprees for Sunday Nimrods.

Maurice Genevoix's "Raboliot" is the archetype of a Sologne poacher, boorish but smart, shaped from the clay of the marshes. As a matter of a fact, the writer wrote this book on the spot, inspired by a local poacher named... Depardieu.

Sologne does not disclose its secrets from the edge of the motorway, nor even during a quick drive through the region. One needs to stop in one of these villages with low brick houses, or at the edge of a pond. This is an autumnal region, of game and mushrooms.

One easily understands, in spite of the domains rising behind barbed wire fences, that Sologne is not a rich region.

Left:
An ornamental sculpture in the château of Villesavin.

applied to Gamay red wines strengthened with a little Pinot Noir, and to Sauvignon and Chardonnay white wines. These two appellations gather once a year in the château's orange grove, in celebration of Saint-Vincent's day.

Sologne, a damp, secret land, teeming with animal life, is an immense protected natural area. And yet, its appearance is

The absence of stone made châteaux and castles a rare sight. Le Moulin is undoubtedly the most representative. In Neuvy, the château of Herbault was raised by Nicolas de Foyal, superintendent of the works in Chambord; a tall construction, bordered with nice outhouses and surrounded by moats. The château of La Ravinière, in Fontaines-en-Sologne, is dated from the beginning of the 16th century. The central building and small pavi-

lions on the wings are adorned with beautiful mullioned windows. The château of La Borde in Vernou-en-Sologne is a Louis XIII style construction, made of brick and stone. The château of Villebourgeon in Neung-sur-Beuvron, dated from 1650, was harmoniously enlarged in the 19th century. It is surrounded by woods and a nice pond.

La Morinière, in Mur-de-Sologne, is small château surrounded by moats, crowned with a strange lantern. The château of Montgiron in Veilleins surrounds a courtyard on three sides: a central building dated from the 18th century, and older wings ending with towers with pepper-boxes.

Romorantin-Lanthenay is the "capital" of Sologne. François I lived resided here in his childhood, as his mother was the widow of the count of Angoulême. It is in Romorantin that in 1499, Anne de Bre-

The château of Le Moulin

With its walls and corner turrets demolished, the stronghold of Le Moulin has become a beautiful residence, that is wide open to the woodland scenery of Sologne. The gate house at the entrance bears marks of the drawbridge's existence. The adjoining guards room displays a beautiful gothic vault. The very tall abode is very refined, adorned with beautiful fireplaces and painted ceilings that have not been altered since the 19th century.

tagne gave birth to her daughter, Claude, who was married to François I, allowing him to complete the annexation of Brittany to the kingdom of France. The king fondly remembered the town, to the point where he elected it as his residence.

The plan drawn by Leonardo da Vinci comprised two twin châteaux separated by a canal, that would welcome water jousting. As we know, Chambord was finally chosen. The château of François I has become a sub-prefecture, and Romorantin has remained a quiet little town, that offers a museum of motor sports. The former spinning trade has receded before tourism.

In November, the "Journées gastronomiques de Sologne" *(Gastronomic days of Sologne)* are a gathering for tourists and good food, which fits in perfectly with the height of the hunting season.

The museum of Sologne is set up in a water mill on the river Sauldre. It presents documents about history, economy, arts and crafts, and of course, hunting. It mentions the 12th Jacquemart tower, the former entrance gate to the town.

The château of Le Moulin.

A totally exotic sight here is the Aliotis aquarium, where one can see a colony of piranhas, and Koï carps: these strange Japanese animals are a collector's item, and are rated according to their "dress", following an intricate hierarchy, which makes some of them disproportionately expensive.

Menetou-sur-Cher is a pretty medieval town that can be visited on foot, from the "rue de l'Enfer" *(Hell Street)* to the "rue du Paradis" *(Paradise street),* and where renowned andouillette is produced: the fair dedicated to it takes place every year on the first week-end of May.

Vierzon is the southern gate of Sologne, and features a church that beautifully fuses a 12th century Romanesque style with later gothic additions. In the 19th century, a large production of porcelain developed here, thriving on the kaolin in the subsoil.

In Saint-Georges-sur-la-Prée, the museum of Ochre is dedicated to this clayey soil, coloured by the action of ferric oxide, and that has been extracted since the Middle Age. It was indeed a renowned pigment used for frescoes and paintings.

In La Ferté-Imbault, which welcomes a large and beautiful brick château that was

93

rebuilt in 1630, an ancestral craft is still practised: the making of birch brooms. Yes indeed, these hard-wearing old brooms, without which witches would travel on foot!

Here begins the land of forests, interspersed with clearings, where villages often count no more than three houses. Nançay is the scene for Alain-Fournier's *Grand Meaulnes* (in which he describes it as "the mysterious village at the furthermost bounds of the earth"), with an imaginary museum for this ghostly character. Sologne is well and truly "the nameless land" where anything can happen, and *Le Grand Meaulnes* was in fact almost named this way. The museum is installed in a room in the château's outhouses, that also house a renowned art gallery. It presents manuscripts and photographs relating to the only novel written by Alain-Fournier, who was killed in action in World War I, at the age of 24. If it only just missed the Goncourt award, *Le Grand Meaulnes* left a durable mark in this century's literature, and is continually dissected and studied... and rediscovered by every generation of teenagers.

This town is also the homeland of the Sablés de Nançay *(Translator's note: "Sablé" biscuits are very similar to shortbread)*, a pastry whose invention is dated from 1953, and is incidentally due to a mistake.

Allegedly, the creation of the famous Tarte Tatin too is due to a mistake made at the beginning of the century in the town of Lamothe-Beuvron. The Demoiselles Tatin's apple tart has travelled around the world, but nothing can compare to tasting it in its birthplace, the Hôtel Tatin, across the street from the station. To right a wrong, let it be said that this upside-down tart, cooked with its pastry upwards and served with its pastry downwards, is an old speciality of Sologne. The Lichonneux Brotherhood of the tarte Tatin jealously makes

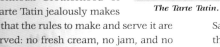

The Tarte Tatin.

sure that the rules to make and serve it are observed: no fresh cream, no jam, and no alcohol!

The simple façade of the château of Argent-sur-Sauldre does not reveal that is a 15th century construction. Nor does it say that it houses a very interesting museum of Popular Crafts and Traditions, in which hours fly by without one noticing them.

In Clémont, the château of Lauroy, which is of course made of brick, is a long and harmonious edifice. The château of Moléon, in Nouan-le-Fuzelier, is surrounded by large moats; its small size does not in the least impair its charming 16th century architecture and beautiful Renaissance dormers.

A road leaving Saint-Viâtre lets one discover many ponds; Saint-Viâtre is a small authentic village, that was once a place of pilgrimage for people suffering from malaria. As to the ponds, they are found here in their hundreds. Ideal ground for hunting, of course, but also for fishing carps, eels and pikes

that are released in them, and that the local gastronomy then prepares so tastily.

La Ferté-Saint-Aubin is renowned for its large château, that also shelters stables and a miniature farm for kids. The old district still features the traditional low-roofed houses of Sologne. To the north, the château of Boisgibault is surrounded by forests; it forms a homogeneous ensemble that dates from the 17th century, and stretches around a courtyard closed by a beautiful gate.

Zoos give visitors the chance to discover nature without any excessive effort; and in the domain of Le Ciran, in Ménestreau-en-Villette, lazier visitors will be content with watching the video, while hikers will grab their boots and binoculars to go and discover the wild fauna of this three-hundred acre park, which has been turned into a showcase of Sologne by the department.

The château of La Ferté-Saint-Aubin

The large château of La Ferté-Saint-Aubin was raised in the 16th century, then greatly enlarged under Louis XIV. It owes its charm to the fortunate juxtaposition of the old castle and a large classical construction. The château, similarly to the long outhouses, is made of brick, a traditional construction material in Sologne. Standing amidst woods, surrounded by large moats, La Ferté is reminiscent of autumn, hunting and fishing... After a time of near abandonment, it has recently been restored to a fine state.

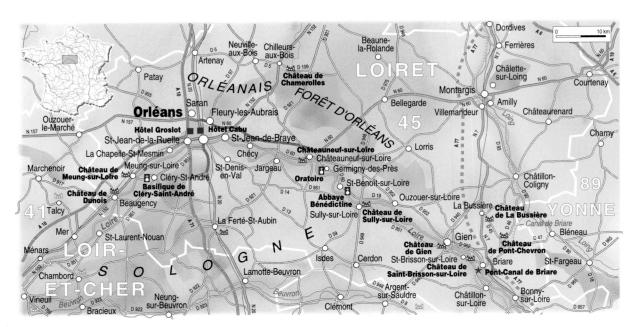

The Loire from Beaugency to Briare

The mayor of Beaugency is lucky indeed! Every day, he enters a town house adorned with a magnificent Renaissance façade, and holds meetings in a room hung with large Louis XIII panels.

The castle of Sully-sur-Loire

It is for having acquired in the year 1602 this castle, that was intended to be a duchy and peerage, that Maximilien de Béthune, superintendent of finances to the court of Henry IV, went down in history under the name of Sully. To the 14th century defensive keep, covered with a roof structure which has survived six centuries ("the finest example of Middle-Age carpentry", according to Viollet-le-Duc), was added the "little castle", remodelled by Sully. Here, he wrote his Memoirs (and had them printed in the château), of which all scholars shall remember that "pasturage and ploughing are the lifeblood of France".

One can visit this castle for the memories of Sully, but also for the site's sheer beauty: few châteaux or castles can claim to have the largest river of France as their moat!

It is in Beaugency that, in the year 1151, a disastrous divorce was spoken: that of king Louis VII and Eleanor of Aquitaine. Two months later indeed, she married Henry Plantagenêt, duke of Normandy, future king of England, and brought him the Aquitaine.

All around, the town of Beaugency offers its fair share of treasures. The castle of Dunois, but also the tower of Saint-Firmin, a tower remaining from the church that was destroyed during the French Revolution. And the beautiful bridge over the Loire, that dates as far back as the 11th century, and that played an important role in the war lead by Joan of Arc against the English.

After the bridge, the Loire riverbanks become wilder. When it reaches Beaugency, the river scatters itself in threads that are often sanded up, making islands rise above the water, where countless birds and a few beavers can be spotted, as they turn small trees into sharp stakes.

The château of Huisseau-sur-Mauves, to the west of Orleans, was reconstructed in the 17th century. It retains several ancient elements, in particular a postern surrounded by towers, and vast kitchens where Joan of Arc stopped before the battle of Patay when, on the 18th June 1429, 4,000 English soldiers were either killed or captured.

The château of Chevilly, standing amongst beautiful forests to the north of Orleans, offers an imposing façade. Its classical chapel offers the sight of remarkable wainscoting.

On the banks of the Loire.

The castle of Dunois

At the heart of the town of Beaugency, the castle of Dunois carries the name of Joan of Arc's faithful companion, who was a bastard of the house of Orleans. The castle was raised by Dunois near the 11th century keep; this keep in fact burnt down during the religious wars, then collapsed in the 19th century, but it still stands! It is now welcomes the museum of popular Art and Traditions of the region of Orleans.

The château of Meung-sur-Loire

Here, the contrast between the pink roughcast 17th century façade, restored and soberly classical, and the medieval towers that rise behind it is rather striking! If the façade can symbolise the residence where the bishops of Orleans resided until the French Revolution, the towers remind us that the castle was also the seat of their justice: dungeons, cells, torture chambers... Amongst many anonymous victims, François Villon tasted ecclesiastical justice here. Unusually enough, it was Louis XI who had him freed.

As it enters the city of Orleans, the river Loire welcomes a tiny affluent: the Loiret, which is only twelve kilometres long, even though it gave its name to the department. Stranger still, this river, which rises from below the ground, is but a reappearance of the Loire! All around, the floral gardens of La Source have vastly grown on the basis the landscaped gardens that were created in the 18th century by an English amateur. From April to September, hundreds of

The floral gardens of la Source.

The basilica of Cléry-Saint-André

In the basilica of Notre-Dame de Cléry rests Louis XI, one of the most debated kings in French history. Religious to the point of superstition, he made the vow to rebuild this ancient shrine, and did so in a flamboyant gothic style that is rather uncommon in the Loire valley. The tombstone of Louis XI dates from 1894; it replaces the tombstone that was raised under Louis XIII and destroyed at the time of the French Revolution, which itself replaced the bronze statue that was stolen by the Huguenots. Louis XI never leaves anyone indifferent!

varieties of flowers bloom, among which no less than eight hundred varieties of irises. This is the favourite strolling place of the inhabitants of Orleans, also offering exhibitions and a butterfly glasshouse.

The Groslot town house

The mayor of Orleans is lucky indeed: he works in one of the most splendid town halls one can find. The Groslot town house was built in 1550, and enlarged in the 19th century. Entirely made of brick, fusing Renaissance and neo-gothic styles, it saw the death of king François II in 1560, after only one year's reign.

Orleans is a large, quiet city which could have been the capital of France. This is where Joan of Arc began her victorious campaign, in the year 1429. Ill-treated during the League wars in the 16th century, Orleans then lost a part of its strategic importance.

The vinegar industry has now replaced the sugar industry (which supplied sugar to half the kingdom) and the unloading of wine for Paris. These wines, which had travelled up the Loire, were sometimes sour by the time they reached Orleans, and were therefore turned into vinegar. Only one company pursues this tradition that consists in maturing flavouring vinegar and maturing it in oak casks.

Rather more pleasant are cotignacs, these very sweet fruit jellies which are a speciality of Orleans. They are sold in wooden boxes bearing the effigy of Joan of Arc, and are prepared according to a truly ancient recipe: one takes nice quinces from which one removes the pips, but keeps the very perfumed skin.

101

The quinces are then moistened in a basin of hot water to make them tender, before being crushed in a sieve. The pulp is then reduced on heat, and poured into an earthenware dish. One adds an equal quantity of sugar, then reduces the mixture on low heat until it clears, before filling moulds of the required shape with it. Finally, the moulds are placed in an oven, the cotignacs are

Right:
The cathedral of Orleans.

The Cabu town house in Orleans

This 16th century town house is remarkable owing to its narrow façade surrounded by two projecting turrets. It houses the historical and archaeological museum of the Orleans region, that presents some magnificent Gallo-Roman bronze animals and figures.

removed from them and sprinkled with sugar.

One easily understands how much easier it is to buy them ready-made! Tallemand des Réaux, a chronicler who lived in the 16th century, and was more attached to small stories than to great history, told that François I, paying a surprise visit to one of his sweethearts, found her in lying her bed... and spotted a lord of the royal Court hiding beneath it! As the sovereign, he took the place due

Orleans, one of the Loire's riverbanks.

to him, but, as a lover he harboured no grudges, and, as a consolation, threw a bag of cotignacs under the bed, laughing: "Well, here you are! Everybody needs to eat!"

The cathedral of Sainte-Croix suffered many torments, even though several Capetians were consecrated within its walls. It was destroyed by Calvinists, and rebuilt by Henry IV, who had just been converted. All the successive centuries left their mark on this beautiful gothic monument. Romanesque art lovers should not fail to visit the respectable church of Saint-Aignan and its crypt with sculpted capitals.

The museum of Fine Arts shelters works by Watteau, Ruysdael, Velasquez, Delacroix, a rich contemporary collection, and especially a high quality pastel production cabinet.

One can also visit Joan of Arc's house, which was reconstituted in... 1965.

On the riverbanks, the Charpenterie market finds shelter beneath strange giant mushrooms that recently grew

thanks to the favours of concrete. Some barges still pass along the Loire, but the harbour activity lies in a deep slumber. The canal of Orleans, that was dug in the 17th century, created a link between the

In the village of Combleux, the canal parallel to the Loire was created in the 17th century.

The château of Chamerolles

This château was recently restored by the department of the Loiret. At the border of the forest of Orleans, this is a beautiful Renaissance château that was built in the 16th century on medieval foundations. One enters it by a drawbridge cast over the moats, to discover a beautiful gallery and, inside, a museum of Perfumes. Behind the château stretch gardens adorned with rare varieties of plants, making Chamerolles a visit that is as instructive as it is distracting.

Châteauneuf-sur-Loir

The "château neuf" (new castle) dated back to the 11th century. It was rebuilt in the 17th century in such a beautiful manner that it was then called the "little Versailles"... before being partly destroyed in the 19th century. Some elements of it remain, sheltering the town hall, an English garden, and the Marine museum of the Loire, which stretches out along the banks where traditional boats are moored.

Loire and the Seine. It is nowadays no longer in use, and its locks stand aligned in Combleux, between the bargemens' houses that rise from the islets.

The Marine museum is set in Château-neuf-sur-Loire, and Tigy, to the south, welcomes the museum of ancient rural crafts.

Tigy also welcomes, every year in May, an asparagus fair. After the siege of Paris in 1870, a demobilised gendarme brought a few crowns of this fine and hard asparagus, which is in fact nothing else than the wild variety "tamed", back from the town of Argenteuil. It is grown in large quantities in the region of Orleans. Its small section makes it ideal for eating as "soldiers" with boiled eggs. Simple, but original and really quite delicious!

To the north of the Loire lies the forest of Orleans, which, with its 40,000 hectares, is France's largest national forest. It was, previously, since the reign of Hugues Capet in 987, a part of the royal domain. It gives shelter to many different animals, and in particular to several rare breeds of birds of prey. It is definitely a quiet, untroubled place to go for a walk.

In Sully-la-Chapelle, at the heart of the forest, the château of Claireau was raised as a marquisate by Louis XV. A beautiful château overlooking the water, adorned with bridges and terraces with balusters. The château of Combreux houses the kennels of a large team of deer hunters. To the north of the forest, the château of Le Hallier is a monumental edifice: walls reinforced by ten large towers, partly filled-in moats behind which Renaissance-era buildings shelter.

The oratory of Germigny-des-Prés

This church dates as far back as Charlemagne! It was initially a small building in the shape of a Greek cross. The addition of a nave, destined to turn it into a parish church, disfigured it, but the plan remains very legible inside the church. Simplicity and contemplation in one of Christianity's most beautiful preserved oratories, that features a beautiful mosaic on the ceiling of one the apses, depicting the hand of God blessing the Ark of the Covenant.

The castle of Bellegarde lies beyond the forest: the large keep, surrounded by water, is more demonstrative than defensive. It is surrounded by nine pavilions scattered throughout the town's public gardens.

Back to the forest of Orleans, to go and smell the scent of Chamerolle. And gourmets will head for Pithiviers, where they can taste a large Danish pastry filled with almond cream or candied fruits. And also some gingerbread, since this is where the recipe was invented. However, one no longer will find any saffron, whose very delicate culture and painstakingly precise picking have brought its culture to an end, whereas in the last century, the Gâtinais region provided 20% of the world's production, sold at a price higher than gold. Indeed, without saffron, goodbye paella, goodbye bouillabaisse, goodbye risotto! In Boynes, a museum tells the story of this culture, that had was introduced by the Romans.

Canal lovers will return via Montargis, which boasts one hundred and twenty six bridges and five rivers, and produces delicious pralines. And tree lovers will return via Nogent-sur-Vernisson and the Arboretum of Les Barres. This property, that belongs to the Vilmorin family (seed merchants) is open to the public. Here, one can discover nearly three thousand breeds of trees from all over the world.

The vineyards in the region of Orleans are found along the Loire, essentially on the left riverbank. The Orleanais once was a prestigious wine, that was served at the tables of Charlemagne and Louis XI, and that was cared for by François I. Nowadays,

Saint-Benoît-sur-Loire

Saint Benoît, founder of occidental monachism, rests in this Benedictine abbey, which acquired great prestige from the seventh century onwards. The convent's buildings disappeared during the French Revolution, but the abbey-church still stands. The Benedictines returned to it in 1944. The imposing porch-tower is a fine example of Romanesque art.

this wine is being rediscovered, just like its neighbour from the Coteaux du Giennois.

This very old vineyard is currently being granted a second birth. It seems that it was first cultivated by the Romans. Served at the Court of Charles V, this wine badly suffered from the phylloxera epidemic in the 19th

The château of Gien

Overlooking the town, the château of Gien, mainly dated from the beginning of the 16th century, was restored after being bombed in 1940, like most of the town. Its façades are covered with bricks laid out geometrically, in the shapes of stars, lozenges and circles; not all have yet unveiled their secrets, but many are probably Masonic references. Gien is a royal château, that was inhabited by Anne de Beaujeu, the daughter of Louis XI and regent queen of France, but also by Henry II, Charles IX and Henry III.

The department of the Loiret has set up a Hunting museum within its walls, that proudly displays hunting collections, and presents a very complete ensemble of works of art by the great wildlife painter François Desportes.

century. The vogue for Sancerre wine let it out of the shadows, and the vineyard, which has actively been replanted these days, now stretches out over more than a hundred hectares, and has obtained an "appellation d'origine contrôlée". Its red, white and "gris" wines marry well with regional pork specialities and cheeses, beginning with the andouillette, which is a speciality in Jargeau, to the east of Orleans. In fact, tradition rather offers a bacon and pork "andouille" *(Translator's note: A larger andouillette),* which is actually... a sausage. Never mind, the "Confrérie du Goûte-Andouille" *(Brotherhood of Andouille tasters)* knows what tastes best! The vineyard of Jargeau was, in times past, renowned for its red wines. Louis XIV stopped, in 1659, at the château of la

The castle of Saint-Brisson-sur-Loire

This 12th century stronghold towering high above the Loire has been altered several times, whilst retaining its six tall towers. The dry moats now welcome medieval war machines that are activated every Sunday in summer!

Queuvre, that is built of brick and stone, and adorned with an exterior helix staircase.

And here come the cheeses: the Olivet, a soft cow's cheese, which Balzac ate with relish. The Pithiviers (not to be confused with the pastry), fairly similar but stronger in taste. And the Vendôme, which is often served coated in wood ash.

The region is one of connoisseurs: Olivet, to the south of Orleans, besides its cheese, has given its name to a cherry variety, and produces pear eau-de-vie *(Translator's note: a strong alcohol, similar to brandy).* In Sully are sold "langues de femmes" *(Women's tongues),* which are thin sweet biscuits with almonds and hazelnuts.

In Gien, the local speciality is thrush pâté.

The town of Gien offers a beautiful view from the riverbanks of the Loire. The château's massive shape overlooks the town, a large part of which was destroyed during a bombing in 1940 — but its reconstruction is a success. Gien is famous throughout the world for its ear-

thenware, produced in a factory that is open to visitors.

In Briare, one once again discovers the complexity of the river network. Here, structures become works of art. Briare also is to thank for an earthenware making process, that was elaborated in the 19th century, and whose

The canal bridge of Briare

Strolling along this bridge, which takes the Briare canal across the river Loire, is a strange experience. This canal, that was created in the 17th century, allowed the Seine to be connected to the Loire. But access to the Loire was dangerous, and it was only in 1896 that the canal bridge was constructed by Gustave Eiffel. To its functionality, this bridge, which is Europe's longest in its category, joins a certain majesty inspired by its decoration: steles, crowned street lamps, tree alignments...
An animated model is featured in the "Maison des deux marines" (House of the two Navies) in Briare, explaining how one formerly crossed the Loire.

story is told in the museum of Mosaics and Earthenware. Briare also produced pearls for necklaces, which were sometimes used as bargaining chips — the notorious jewellery that was used by explorers in African lands.

The château of Pont-Chevron

Who would believe, upon seeing this large classical Louis XVI style residence, with a rounded forepart and two slightly projecting wings, rising at the far end of vast flower beds, that Pont-Chevron had been built in 1900? And yet, this is the case. The Harcourt family is to thank for this fine realisation.

The château of La Bussière

The château of La Bussière was once at the heart of a very large farming domain, as the huge grain lofts standing here testify to, constructed in pink-coloured brick with black lozenges. The Louis XIII style château overlooks a pond, and is surrounded by gardens planned by Le Nôtre. The 19th century alterations have changed nothing to the place's magic.
The château is also a Fishing museum offering countless instruments, sketches, table objects, and even a rare stuffed coelacanth. This fish, which has not changed in the space of 400 million years, was discovered near the Comoro Islands, in 1938.

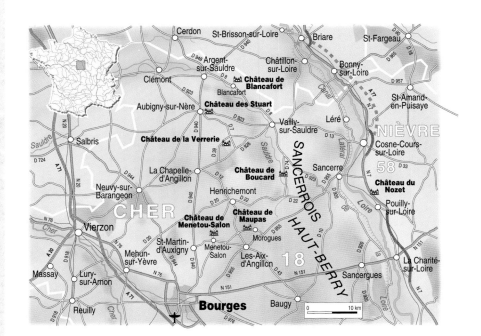

The château of Blancafort

A nice 15th century château that was later partly rebuilt. Its fortified residence appearance, which is mainly due to its corner turrets, has been "softened" by a gallery with arcades and a formal garden. This private château is adorned with beautiful furniture.

The Sancerrois and the pays Fort

This is a land of vineyards, of course. But also a land of forests, that are more welcoming than their names suggest. And the Sancerrois region, between Sologne and Berry, is a mysterious region. Witchcraft indeed is a traditional image that

The vineyards of Sancerre.

clings to the Berry, and which can be "conjured" by a visit to the museum dedicated to it by the town of Blancafort. Does witchcraft have a present, a future? These facts are not stated in any tourist guide.

The "Petit-Château" *(Small castle)*, in Autry-le-Chatel, doesn't deserve its name built on the ruins of another castle, it is a rather well-developed construction, with a long abode and two round towers. At the other end of the forest of Brisson, the town of Beaulieu-sur-Loire welcomes the château of Courcelles, that was rebuilt in the 17th century on medieval founda-

The château of the Stuarts

The château of the Stuarts is nowadays the town hall of Aubigny-sur-Nère. Of the 16th century construction remain a beautiful entrance gate house and two wings of the château. Here, one can visit the museum of the French-Scottish Alliance. The gardens are said to have been planned by Le Nôtre.

tions; and the château of Assay, that was given to Scots in 1430 by king Charles VII. In spite of later additions, it retains a medieval appearance: drawbridge, postern, and rampart walk.

As we travel along the Loire, we stumble upon Villattes, constructed in the 15th century by the Count of Nevers, that presents a polygonal tower and sculpted windows.

Then Buranlure, in the region of Boulleret, which has not been altered in the slightest since its construction in the 15th century. This is a fine rural edifice, crowned with brick, organised around a closed-in yard which can be accessed via a drawbridge.

And the château of Le Peseau, which has kept, behind a defensive gate house, some fine 18th century buildings.

Aubigny-sur-Nère is Scottish land in the region of Sologne. This rather original situation is a consequence of the alliance of Charles VII, Joan of Arc's king, with the Scots, the appointed enemies of the English. As a reward for their help, the

The château of La Verrerie

Another construction by the Scottish Stuarts, the château of La Verrerie stands amidst nice lands. Constructions range from the 15th to the 19th century, but form a homogeneous ensemble, that is emphasised by a fine Renaissance gallery.

Stuarts were given this town and its castle, that formerly belonged to the Capetian domain.

The Scottish dynasty did not leave Aubigny before the 19th century. And what remains? Beautiful houses with wooden sides, that were built after a fire in the 16th century. Memories of the duchess of Portsmouth, friend of Louis XIV and mistress of the king of England, Charles II. A museum of the French-Scottish Alliance. The July celebrations, when the town's inhabitants wear kilts. And, further, the château of La Verrerie.

Henri Alban Fournier was born in La Chapelle-d'Angillon, where the château houses a museum dedicated to him. Killed

Aubigny-sur-Nère.

117

*ci **Henri IV** offrit à une jeune bergère un gobelet d'eau en lui disant "Boisbelle"*

The château of Boucard

A peaceful castle, whose primitive fortress appearance is attenuated by the Renaissance courtyard and the opening of the walls to the grounds. Facing the gate house overlooking the old drawbridge, one enters the château by a bridge overstepping the moats. In the summer, the château welcomes classical music concerts.

in Word War I at the young age of 24, he only signed one novel — but what a novel! *"Le Grand Meaulnes"* —, in which romantic love fades among the mists of Sologne.

La Chapelle-d'Angillon was once also a freehold: the independent principality of Boisbelle, which struck coins, had gained recognition from the kings of France, and had been owned by illustrious people: Diane de La Marck, the heroine of *"The Princess of Cleves"*. And Sully, who acquired Boisbelle in 1605 and founded its capital in Henrichemont, named Henrici-Mons honour of Henry IV: independence should not replace circumspection!

Henrichemont is built in the shape of a compass rose. The tanneries that once ensured the town's prosperity have now disappeared. Today, one finds a pottery specialised in monumental pieces.

As in La Borne, where earth has been cooked since the 13th century. A hundred years ago, there were nearly one hundred potters. Today, only half of these remain, which isn't so bad! The small village of course counts many workshops, exhibitions, and the Ivanoff museum, which exhibits the works of a modern ceramist who had a workshop in town. More classi-

cal pieces are presented in a second museum.

In the pays Fort, prairies are closed-in by quickset hedges, and many rivers flow through the land. It is a land of forests and copses. Of orchards too, as around Saint-Martin-d'Auxigny, a region that is called the Terreville. Apple and pear trees, that are covered with canvas sheets in summer, trace arabesques throughout the hills.

In Menetou-Salon, one comes to visit the château, that was rebuilt in the 19th century, but also a strange oil-lamp

The château of Maupas

A large five-storey tower, dated from the 15th century, overlooks the château of Maupas, that is set amongst forests. The château's staircase is a connoisseur indeed: it is adorned with 900 earthenware plates from all around the world.

museum. And, of course, the vineyard! Over 300 hectares, it produces fine Pinot Noir red wines, and especially white wines that are best kept for a few years, vigorous, silky, sometimes firmer in taste than Sancerre wines. The "village de Morogues" is a renowned vintage.

The vineyards become more interspersed to the east, where they meet the Sancerre vineyards.

The glory of Sancerre wine is universal, and the 2300 hectares of vine aren't always enough to meet the demand. These wines bear the mark of the different soils that share the hilltops as they reach up towards the town. Sancerre is a wine of immediate pleasure, dry, full, supple and nonetheless lively. It provides marvellous accompaniment to fishes and goat's cheeses, of which the most famous is the "Crottin de Chavignol", which has been given an "appellation contrôlée".

This goat's cheese comes as small, flattened balls, slightly rounded at the centre, with a fine and regular crust, that can be covered with white or blue mould. Its texture can range from creamy, when it is fresh, to brittle, when it is dry.

Sancerre is a small town, considering the great flood of people that invades it in the summer months. Narrow alleyways intersect, leading to a few small squares with differences in level that can be fero-

cious! The castle ruins overlook this maze; the castle was raised in 1153 by Etienne de Champagne, the first count of Sancerre. The town, when it became Huguenot, was under siege for six

Below:
The village of Sancerre.

The château of Menetou-Salon

The 19th century is indeed attractive when, as is the case here, it gives such a perfectly mastered reading of the Renaissance! Nothing remains of the stronghold that was built in the 5th century. Alterations from the last century aimed to recapture the atmosphere of the times of Jacques Cœur, who owned the château in the 15th century. The grounds feature a maze of gothic inspiration. The inside of the château is richly furnished, as a prince's residence should be. The stables now house a museum of old-time vehicles that have been gathered by the prince of Arenberg, the owner of the château.

Specialities of Sancerre.

months. Finally, both castle and fortifications were razed to the ground.

One travels to Sancerre for the beauty of the landscapes and the freshness of the cellars. And also for Sancerre's cakes, croquettes and "lichoux".

One can feel that Burgundy lies near, in fact only a crossing of the Loire away. But the vineyard of Pouilly nonetheless remains part of the Loire region. The vine grown here is the Sauvignon, as in Sancerre. The Pouilly-Fumé left the meanest share to the Pouilly-sur-Loire, which grows Chasselas vines.

The Pouilly-Fumé is a firm high-class wine, that benefits from ageing a few years. Good vintages are left to mature in wooden casks, in order to increase the wine's vigour.

A final trip to the left riverbank gives us the opportunity to salute the château of La Grange-Montalivet, that was built around the year 1600. The abode is crowned with a dome and surrounded by two identical pavilions, that face beautiful grounds.

The château of Le Nozet

Standing near the Loire, but already a part of the region of Bourgogne, the château of Le Nozet is the last stop in our journey. It is a pure 19th century creation, built over a former 15th century manor, that teems with neo-gothic quotations. This fine château, surrounded by flower beds and vast grounds, is the centre of a renowned Pouilly-Fumé vineyard.

And one last crossing over to the right riverbank to salute the large château of Mesvres-sur-Loire, a neo-Renaissance style of

architecture whose secrets were only ever revealed by the second Empire... and now we leave the great river, whose banks still travel far upstream, as far as the Massif central. It is from these high and depopulated lands that the Loire flows, growing bigger inch by inch thanks to streams, as it brings water to the basin where the history of France was so often decided of, for the greater benefit of all amateurs of beautiful châteaux.

The Loire in Pouilly.

THE ANGEVIN LOIRE

• CHÂTEAU OF SERRANT.
Château of Serrant. 49170 Saint-Georges-sur-
Loire. Visits, April to December.
Phone: 02.41.39.13.01.
• CHÂTEAU OF LE PLESSIS-MACÉ, 49770 Le Plessis-
Macé. Visits, March to November, every day
except Tuesday. Phone: 02.41.32.67.93.
• CHÂTEAU OF BRISSAC,
49320 Brissac-Quincié. Visits, April to
October. Phone: 02.41.91.22.21.
• WORKSHOP OF THE PAINTER RICHARD RACK.
Manor of La Caillère, 49320 Coutures. Visits,
May to September. Phone: 02.41.57.97.97.
• CHÂTEAU OF MONTGEOFFROY, 49250 Mazé.
Visits, Palm Sunday to All Saints' Day.
Phone: 02.41.80.60.02.
• CHÂTEAU OF SAUMUR,
49400 Saumur. Visits, all year round, except
Tuesday. Phone: 02.41.40.24.40.
• CAVES BOUVET-LADUBAY (WINE CELLARS).
49400 Saint-Hilaire-Saint-Florent. Visits,...
Phone: 02.41.83.83.83
• CASTLE OF MONTREUIL-BELLAY,
49260 Montreuil-Bellay. Visits, April to
October. Phone: 02.41.52.33.06.
• CHÂTEAU OF MONTSOREAU,
49730 Montsoreau. Visits, all year round
(except between 1st and 15th March and
15th and 30th November), every day except
Tuesday. Phone: 02.41.51.70.25
• CHÂTEAU OF LE BREIL DE FOIN,
49490 Genneteil. Visits, from mid-July to the
end of August. Phone: 02.41.82.25.13.
• ABBEY OF FONTEVRAUD.
49590 Fontevraud-l'Abbaye. Visits, every
day. Phone: 02.41.51.71.41.

TRAVELLING UP THE LOIR VALLEY

• CHÂTEAU OF LE PLESSIS-BOURRÉ,
49460 Ecuillé. Visits, from January to 15th
November, closed on Wednesdays.
Phone: 02.41.32.06.01.
• CHÂTEAU OF DURTAL, 49430 Durtal. Visits,
from February to December, closed on
Tuesdays. Phone: 02.41.76.31.37.
• MAISON DE LA TERRE CUITE (EARTHENWARE
COLLECTION). Route de Fougeré, 49340 Les
Rairies. Visits, from June to August.
Phone: 02.41.76.33.12.
• FAÏENCERIES D'ART DE MALICORNE (ART
EARTHENWARE WORKSHOPS AND FACTORY).
18 rue Bernard-Palissy, 72270 Malicorne.
Visits, from Easter to September.
Phone: 02.43.94.81.18.
• CHÂTEAU OF BAZOUGES, 72200 Bazouges-sur-
le-Loir. Visits, from 15th June to 15th
September. Phone: 02.43.45.32.62.
• MOULIN DE LA BRUÈRE (WATER MILL),
72000 La Flèche. Visits on saturdays
Phone: 02.43.94.45.64.
• MOULIN DE ROTROU (WATER MILL),
72500 Vaas. Visits, from Easter to October.
Phone: 02.43.46.70.22.
• CHÂTEAU OF LE LUDE, 72800 Le Lude.
Visits, from April to September.
Phone: 02.43.94.60.09.

• CENTRE D'ARTISANAT D'ART DES MOULINS DE
PAILLARD (ARTS AND HANDICRAFTS CENTRE).
72340 Poncé-sur-Loir. Visits, every day
except Monday. Phone: 02.43.44.45.31.
• CHÂTEAU OF PONCÉ,
72340 Poncé sur le Loir. Visits, from April to
September. Phone: 02.43.44.45.39.
• CHÂTEAU OF COURTANVAUX, 72310 Bessé-sur-
Braye. Visits, from 15th May to
30th September, closed on Tuesdays.
Phone: 02.43.35.34.43.
• MANOR OF LA POSSONNIÈRE, 41800 Coutures-
sur-Loir. Visits, on weekends, from 1st April
to 15th November, every day except Monday
and Tuesday in summer.
Phone: 02.54.72.40.05.
• PARC BOTANIQUE DE LA FOSSE (BOTANICAL
GARDEN), 1800 Fontaine-les-Coteaux. Visits,
from Easter to the end of September, closed
on Mondays and Tuesdays.
Phone: 02.54.85.38.63.
• PARC BOTANIQUE DE ROC EN TUF (BOTANICAL
GARDEN), 41800 Ternay. Visits, from May to
September. Phone: 02.54.72.57.03.
• PARC ET JARDIN DU DOMAINE DE SASNIÈRES
(DOMAIN GROUNDS AND GARDEN),
41310 Sasnières. Visits, from May to October.
Phone: 02.54.82.92.34.
• CHÂTEAU OF LE FRESNE, 41310 Authon.
Visits, from mid-June to mid-August.
Phone: 02.54.80.33.04.
• TRAIN TOURISTIQUE DE LA VALLÉE DU LOIR
(SIGHTSEEING TRAIN). Thoré-la-Rochette
railway station. Visits, on weekends, from
June to August. Phone: 02.54.72.80.82.
• CHÂTEAU OF LA MÉZIÈRE, La Praizerie,
41360 Lunay. Visits, from Easter to
September. Phone: 02.54.72.04.15.
• CHAMPIGNONNIÈRE DU VAL SAINT-ANDRÉ
(MUSHROOM BEDS), 1100 Villier-sur-Loir. Visits,
all year round. Phone: 02.54.72.78.10.

IN THE HOMELAND OF RABELAIS,
FROM CHINON TO RICHELIEU

• CASTLE OF CHINON, 37500 Chinon. Visits,
every day. Phone: 02.47.93.13.45.
• MUSÉE DU VIEUX CHINON ET DE LA BATELLERIE
(MUSEUM OF ANCIENT CHINON AND OF RIVER AND
CANAL CRAFT), 44 rue Haute-Saint-Maurice,
37500 Chinon. Visits, from Easter to All
Saints' Day. Phone: 02.47.93.18.12.
• MUSÉE DU VIN ET DE LA TONNELLERIE
(MUSEUM OF WINE AND COOPERAGE),
12 rue Voltaire, 37500 Chinon. Visits, April
to September. Phone: 02.47.93.25.63.
• LA DEVINIÈRE, 37500 Seuilly. Visits, every
day. Phone: 02.47.95.91.18.
• CHÂTEAU OF USSÉ, 7420 Rigny-Ussé. Visits,
from February to 11th November.
Phone: 02.47.95.54.05.
• POIRES TAPÉES DE RIVARENNE (RIVARENNE
"TAPPED" PEARS). 37190 Rivarenne.
Phone: 02.47.95.47.78.
• TRAIN À VAPEUR DE CHINON À RICHELIEU
(STEAM TRAIN RUNNING FROM CHINON TO
RICHELIEU). Runs from June to September.
Phone: 02.47.58.12.97.

- DOMAINE DE LA PATAUDIÈRE,
37120 Champigny-sur-Veule. Truffle fields.
Phone: 02.47.58.12.15.
- CHÂTEAU OF LE GRAND-PRESSIGNY,
37350 Le Grand-Pressigny. Visits, from
February to November.
Phone: 02.47.94.90.20.
- MUSÉE DESCARTES (MUSEUM DEDICATED TO
DESCARTES), 29 rue Descartes,
37160 Descartes. Visits, from mid-January to
mid-November, closed on Tuesdays.
Phone: 02.47.59.79.19.

THE ROYAL LOIRE, FROM BOURGUEIL TO AMBOISE

- ABBEY OF BOURGUEIL, 37140 Bourgueil.
Visits, on weekends, from April to October,
also on Mondays and Thursdays in summer.
Phone: 02.47.97.72.04.
- CHÂTEAU OF LES RÉAUX, 37140 Chouzé-sur-
Loire. Visits of the grounds, all year round.
Bed and Breakfast. Phone: 02.47.95.14.40.
- CHÂTEAU OF GIZEUX, 37340 Gizeux. Visits,
from June to September.
Phone: 02.47.96.50.92.
- CHÂTEAU OF CHAMPCHEVRIER,
7340 Cléré-les-Pins. Visits, April to
September. Phone: 02.47.24.93.93.
- CASTLE OF LANGEAIS. 37130 Langeais. Visits,
every day except Christmas day.
Phone: 02.47.96.72.60.
- CHÂTEAU OF VILLANDRY, 37510 Villandry.
Visits, all year round. Phone: 02.47.50.02.09.
- GROTTES PÉTRIFIANTES DE SAVONNIÈRES
(LIMESTONE CAVES), 37510 Savonnières. Visits,
from February to December.
Phone: 02.47.50.00.09.
- CASTLE OF LUYNES, 37230 Luynes. Visits,
from mid-March to the end of September.
Phone: 02.47.55.67.55.
- CHÂTEAU OF PLESSIS-LES-TOURS
PRIEURÉ SAINT-COSME (PRIORY), 37520 La
Riche. Visits, from February to November.
Phone: 02.47.37.32.70.
- THE ARCHIEPISCOPAL PALACE OF TOURS
LE ROYAL CHÂTEAU OF TOURS
THE GOÜIN TOWN HOUSE IN TOURS
HISTORIAL DE TOURAINE (HISTORICAL PANORAMA
OF TOURAINE), MUSÉE GRÉVIN, 25 avenue
André-Malraux, 37000 Tours. Visits, all year
round. Phone: 02.47.61.02.95.
- SAINT-MARTIN MUSEUM, 3 rue Rapin,
37000 Tours. Visits, from mid-March to mid-
November. Phone: 02.47.05.68.73.
- MUSÉE DU COMPAGNONNAGE (MUSEUM OF
TRADE GUILDS), 8 rue Nationale, 37000 Tours.
Visits, every day, except Tuesday in the low
season. Phone: 02.47.61.07.93.
- MUSÉE DU GEMMAIL (MUSEUM OF NON-LEADED
STAINED GLASS), 7 rue du Mûrier, 37000 Tours.
Visits, every day, from April to
15th November, and on weekends all year
round. Phone: 02.47.61.01.19
- MUSÉE DE LA COIFFE ET BRODERIES DE
TOURAINE (MUSEUM OF TOURAINE HEADDRESSES
AND EMBROIDERIES), 68 quai de Loire,
37210 Rochecorbon. Visits, every day.
Phone: 02.47.52.80.16.

- MANOR OF LES BASSES-RIVIÈRES,
37210 Rochecorbon. Visits, from Easter
weekend to September, every day except
Tuesday in July and August.
Phone: 02.47.52.80.99.
- LA GRANGE DE MESLAY (BARN OF MESLAY),
37210 Parçay-Meslay. Visits, on weekends,
from Easter to All Saints' Day.
Phone: 02.47.29.19.29.
- ESPACE DE LA VIGNE ET DU VIN (CENTRE OF
VIN AND WINE). 37210 Vouvray. Visits, every
day. Phone: 02.47.52.76.00.
- CHÂTEAU OF JALLANGES, 37210 Vernou-sur-
Brenne. Visits, from 15th March to 15th
October. Phone: 02.47.52.01.71.
- THE GARDENS OF VALMER, 37210 Chancay.
Visits, on weekends from May to September,
every day except Monday in summer.
Phone: 02.47.52.93.12.
- CHÂTEAU OF LA BOURDAISIÈRE,
37270 Montlouis-sur-Loire. Visits, from mid-
March to mid-November.
Phone: 02.47.45.16.31.
- CHÂTEAU OF AMBOISE, 37400 Amboise.
Visits, every day. Phone: 02.47.57.00.98.
- HÔTEL DE JOYEUSE ET MUSÉE DE LA POSTE
(THE JOYEUSE TOWN HOUSE AND POST OFFICE
MUSEUM), 6 rue de Joyeuse, 37400 Amboise.
Visits, April to September.
Phone: 02.47.57.00.11.
- LE CLOS-LUCÉ (MANOR), 37400 Amboise.
Visits, every day. Phone: 02.47.57.62.88.
- LA MAISON ENCHANTÉE (THE ENCHANTED
HOUSE), 7 rue du Général-Foy,
37400 Amboise. Visits, every day, except
Monday in winter. Phone: 02.47.23.24.50.
- PAGODE DE CHANTELOUP (PAGODA OF
CHANTELOUP), 37400 Amboise. Visits, from
mid-February to mid-November, every day.
Phone: 02.47.57.20.97.
- AQUARIUM OF TOURAINE,
37400 Lussault-sur-Loire. Visits, from April
to mid-November. Phone: 02.47.23.44.44.
- PARC DES MINI-CHÂTEAUX (PARK OF MINIATURE
CASTLES AND CHÂTEAUX), 37400 Amboise.
Visits, from April to mid-November.
Phone: 02.47.23.44.44.
- LE FOU DE L'ANE (THE "DONKEY CRAZE"),
37400 Amboise. Visits, from April to mid-
November. Phone: 02.47.23.44.44.

THE VALLEY OF THE INDRE

- CHÂTEAU OF AZAY-LE-RIDEAU,
7190 Azay-le-Rideau. Visits, every day.
Phone: 02.47.45.42.04.
- MUSÉE MAURICE-DUFRESNE (MUSEUM).
Marnay, 37190 Azay-le-Rideau. Visits, every
day. Phone: 02.47.45.36.18.
- COOPÉRATIVE DE VANNERIE (CANEWORK
COOPERATIVE), rue de la Cheneillère,
37190 Villaines-les-Rochers. Visits, every
day. Phone: 02.47.45.43.03.
- CHÂTEAU OF SACHÉ, 7190 Saché. Visits, from
February to November. Phone: 02.47.26.86.50.
- LABYRINTHE VÉGÉTAL (MAZE), RN 143, 37310
Reignac-sur-Indre. Visits, from 10th July to
the end of August. Phone: 02.47.42.63.62.

ADDRESSES

• CHÂTEAU ET DONJON DE LOCHES (THE CHÂTEAU AND ITS KEEP), 37600 Loches. Visits, every day from February to November. Phone: 02.47.59.01.32.
• CARRIÈRE TROGLODYTIQUE DE VIGNEMONT (TROGLODYTIC QUARRY), 52 ter rue des Roches, 37600 Loches. Visits, from Easter to All Saints' Day. Phone: 02.47.91.54.54.
• CASTLE OF MONTRÉSOR, 37460 Montrésor. Visits, from April to November. Phone: 02.47.92.60.04.

THE CHER VALLEY

• CHÂTEAU OF NITRAY, 37270 Athée-sur-Cher. Visits, from mid-June to mid-September. Phone: 02.47.50.60.48.
• CHÂTEAU OF CHENONCEAU, 37150 Chenonceaux. Visits, every day. Phone: 02.47.23.90.07.
• DISTILLERIE FRAISE OR (DISTILLERY), between Chissey et Chisseau, 41400 Chissay. Visits, from Easter to the end of September. Phone: 02.54.32.32.05.
• CHÂTEAU OF MONTPOUPON, 37460 Céré-la-Ronde. Visits, on weekends, from April to October, every day from 15th June to the end of September. Phone: 02.47.94.23.62
• CAVES MONMOUSSEAU ET MUSÉE DES CONFRÉRIES EUROPÉENNES (MONMOUSSEAU WINE CELLARS AND MUSEUM OF EUROPEAN BROTHERHOODS), road to Vierzon, 41400 Montrichard. Visits from April to November. Phone: 02.54.71.66.66.
• DONJON DES AIGLES (KEEP OF THE EAGLES), château of Montrichard, 41400 Montrichard. Shows from mid-May to mid-September. Phone: 02.54.32.01.16.
• CAVES CHAMPIGNONNIÈRES (CELLARS SHELTERING MUSHROOM BEDS), 40 route des Roches, 41400 Bourré. Visits, from Palm Sunday to the end of November. Phone: 02.54.32.35.15.
• LA MAGNANERIE (THE SILKWORM COCOONERY), chemin de la Croix-Barbin, 41400 Bourré. Visits, in summer. Phone: 02.54.32.63.91.
• MUSÉE DU CHOCOLAT (MUSEUM OF CHOCOLATE), abbey of Pontlevoy, 41400 Pontlevoy. Visits, from Palm Sunday to All Saints' Day. Phone: 02.54.32.60.80.
• CHÂTEAU OF LE GUÉ-PÉAN, 41400 Monthou-sur-Cher. Visits, all year round. Phone: 02.54.71.43.01.
• MUSÉE ARCHÉOLOGIQUE (ARCHAEOLOGICAL MUSEUM), 41140 Thésée-la-Romaine. Visits, de mid-June to mid-September, closed on Tuesdays, on weekends in the low season. Phone: 02.54.71.40.20.
• CHÂTEAU OF CHÉMERY, 41700 Chémery. Visits, from March to November. Phone: 02.54.71.82.77.
• CHÂTEAU OF SELLES-SUR-CHER, 41130 Selles-sur-Cher. Visits, from Easter to All Saints' Day. Phone: 02.54.97.63.98.
• CHÂTEAU OF VALENCAY, 36600 Valençay. Visits, every day from 15th March to 15th November and on weekends in the low season. Phone: 02.54.00.10.66.

• MUSÉE SUCRÉ DE LA PÂTISSERIE CHICHERY (THE SWEET MUSEUM OF CHICHERY PASTRIES AND CAKES), 21 rue du Château, 36600 Valençay. Closed on Mondays. Phone: 02.54.00.12.13.
• CHÂTEAU OF BOUGES, Bouges-le-Château. Visits, from April to October except on Tuesdays, every day in July and August. Phone: 02.54.35.88.26.

THE LOIRE OF BLOIS
AND CHAMBORD

• CHÂTEAU OF CHAUMONT-SUR-LOIRE, 41150 Chaumont-sur-Loire. Visits, every day. Phone: 02.54.51.26.26.
• CASTLE OF FOUGÈRES-SUR-BIÈVRE, 41120 Fougères-sur-Bièvre. Visits, all year round, except on Tuesdays, from October to March. Phone: 02.54.20.27.18.
• CHÂTEAU OF ROUJOUX, route de Fougères, 41700 Fresnes. Visits, from April to All Saints' Day. Phone: 02.54.79.53.55.
• CHÂTEAU OF BEAUREGARD, 41120 Cellettes. Visits, from May to October. Phone: 02.54.70.40.05.
• CHÂTEAU OF CHAMBORD. 41250 Chambord. Visits, every day. Phone: 02.54.50.40.00.
• YAM PRODUCTION AND SALE, AND EXPLANATIONS ABOUT THEIR CULTURE. GAEC Huguet, 12 rue de La Franchetière, 41 Saint-Claude-de-Diray. Phone: 02.54.20.57.36.
• ROYAL CHÂTEAU OF BLOIS. 41000 Blois. Visits, every day. Phone: 02.54.78.06.62. Son et lumière show from mid-May to mid-September.
• MAISON DE LA MAGIE ROBERT-HOUDIN (ROBERT HOUDIN HOUSE OF MAGIC), 1 place du Château, 41000 Blois. Visits, from June to September. Phone: 02.54.55.26.26.
• MUSÉE DE L'OBJET (MUSEUM OF OBJECTS), 6 rue Franciade, 41000 Blois. Visits, on weekends, and from Wednesday to Sunday in summer. Phone: 02.54.78.87.26.
• MUSÉE DES BEAUX-ARTS (MUSEUM OF FINE ARTS), n the château
Haras national de Blois (National stud farm of Blois), 41000 Blois. Visits, from 15th March to 15th November, closed on Sundays. Phone: 02.54.55.22.82.
• MUSÉUM D'HISTOIRE NATURELLE (MUSEUM OF NATURAL HISTORY), rue Anne-de-Bretagne, 41000 Blois. Visits, all year round. Phone: 02.54.90.21.00..
• CHÂTEAU OF TALCY, 41370 Talcy. Visits, every day, except Tuesdays in the low season. Phone: 02.54.81.03.01.

SOLOGNE

• CHÂTEAU OF VILLESAVIN, 41250 Tour-en-Sologne. Visits, from March to December. Phone: 02.54.46.42.88.
• CHÂTEAU OF CHEVERNY, 41700 Cheverny. Visits, every day. Phone: 02.54.79.96.29.
• Château of Troussay, 41700 Cheverny. Visits, from June to September, on Sundays in the low season. Phone: 02.54.44.29.07.

• BERGERIES DE SOLOGNE (SHEEPFOLDS OF SOLOGNE). Ferme du Jaugeny. 41250 Fontaines-en-Sologne. Visits, all year round. Phone: 02.54.46.45.61.
• CHÂTEAU OF LE MOULIN, 41230 Lassay-sur-Croisne. Visits, from March to 15th November. Phone: 02.54.83.83.51.
• MUSÉE DE SOLOGNE (MUSEUM OF SOLOGNE). Moulin du Chapitre, 41200 Romorantin-Lanthenay. Visits, every day except Tuesdays. Phone: 02.54.95.33.66.
• AQUARIUM ALIOTIS. Moulin des Tourneux, 41200 Villeherviers. Visits, all year round. Phone: 02.54.95.26.26.
• MUSÉE DE L'OCRE (MUSEUM OF OCHRE), 18100 Saint-Georges-sur-la-Prée. Visits, Friday to Sunday from March to December, also on Mondays and Thursdays in summer. Phone: 02.48.52.00.20.
• MUSÉE IMAGINAIRE DU GRAND MEAULNES (IMAGINARY MUSEUM OF LE GRAND MEAULNES). 18330 Nancay. Visits, on weekends from mid-March to mid-December. Phone: 02.48.51.80.22.
• MUSÉE DES MÉTIERS (MUSEUM OF CRAFTS), château of Argent-sur-Sauldre, 18410 Argent-sur-Sauldre. Visits from Easter to All Saints' Day, closed on Tuesdays. Phone: 02.48.73.33.10.
• CHÂTEAU OF LA FERTÉ-SAINT-AUBIN, 45240 La Ferté-Saint-Aubin. Visits, every day from 15th February to 15th November. Phone: 02.38.76.52.72.
• DOMAINE DE CIRAN, 45240 Menestreau-en-Villette. Visits, from October to March, closed on Tuesdays. Phone: 02.38.76.90.93.

THE LOIRE, FROM BEAUGENCY TO BRIARE

• TOWN HALL OF BEAUGENCY. 45190 Beaugency. Visits, on request. Phone: 02.38.44.50.01..
• CASTLE OF DUNOIS, 45190 Beaugency. Visits, every day, except Tuesdays: 02.38.44.55.23.
• CHÂTEAU OF MEUNG-SUR-LOIRE, 45130 Meung-sur-Loire. Visits, every day. Phone: 02.38.44.36.47.
• GROSLOT TOWN HOUSE, place de l'Etape, 45000 Orléans. Visits, every day. Phone: 02.38.79.22.30.
• CABU TOWN HOUSE, square Anné-Desnoyer, 45000 Orléans. Visits, on Wednesdays, Saturdays, Sundays, and from Tuesday to Sunday from May to September. Phone: 02.38.79.25.60.
• MUSEUM OF FINE ARTS, place Sainte-Croix, 45000 Orléans. Visits, every day except Tuesdays. Phone: 02.38.53.39.22.
• MUSÉE DE L'ARTISANAT RURAL ANCIEN (MUSEUM OF ANCIENT RURAL CRAFTS), 60 rue de Sully, 45510 Tigy. Visits, on Sundays, from Easter to All Saints' Day, also on Saturdays in summer. Phone: 02.38.58.00.42.
• CHÂTEAU OF CHAMEROLLES, 45170 Chilleurs-aux-Bois. Visits, from February to December, closed on Fridays. Phone: 02.38.39.84.66.
• MAISON DU SAFRAN (SAFFRON HOUSE), 45300 Boynes. Visits, on weekends, from April to October. Phone: 02.38.33.13.05.
• ARBORETUM OF LES BARRES, 45290 Nogent-sur-Vernisson. Visits, from mid-March to mid-November. Phone: 02.38.97.62.21.

• CHÂTEAU OF CHÂTEAUNEUF-SUR-LOIR, 45110 Châteauneuf-sur-Loir. Visits, every day, except Tuesdays from November to March. Phone: 02.38.58.44.79.
• BASILICA OF SAINT-BENOÎT-SUR-LOIRE, 45730 Saint-Benoît-sur-Loire. Visits, every day. Phone: 02.38.35.79.00.
• CASTLE OF SULLY-SUR-LOIRE, 45600 Sully-sur-Loire. Visits, from March to November. Phone: 02.38.36.36.86.
• CHÂTEAU OF GIEN, 45500 Gien. Visits, every day except Mondays. Phone: 02.38.67.69.69.
• MUSÉE DE LA FAÏENCERIE DE GIEN (GIEN MUSEUM OF EARTHENWARE), place de la Victoire, 45500 Gien. Visits, every day. Phone: 02.38.67.00.05.
• CASTLE OF SAINT-BRISSON, 45500 Saint-Brisson. Visite, de Pâques au 15 novembre, sauf mardi. Téléphone : 02.38.36.71.29.
• MAISON DES DEUX MARINES (HOUSE OF THE TWO NAVIES), 58 boulevard Buyser, 45250 Briare. Visits, from March to December. Phone: 02.38.31.28.27.
• MUSÉE DE LA MOSAÏQUE ET DES EMAUX (MUSEUM OF MOSAICS AND EARTHENWARE), boulevard Loreau, 45250 Briare. Visits, from March to December. Phone: 02.38.31.20.51.
• CHÂTEAU OF PONT-CHEVRON, 45250 Ouzouer-sur-Trézée. Visits, from mid-March to mid-September, closed on Tuesdays. Phone: 02.38.31.92.02.
• CHÂTEAU OF LA BUSSIÈRE, 45230 La Bussière. Visits, from April to October. Phone: 02.38.35.93.35.

THE SANCERROIS AND THE PAYS FORT

• MUSÉE DE LA SORCELLERIE (MUSEUM OF WITCHCRAFT). La Jonchère, 18410 Concressault. Visits, from Easter to October. Phone: 02.48.73.86.11.
• CHÂTEAU OF BLANCAFORT, 18410 Blancafort. Visits, from 15th March to 11th November, closed on Tuesdays. Phone: 02.48.58.60.56.
• CHÂTEAU OF LA VERRERIE, 18700 Oizon. Visits, from March to November. Phone: 02.48.58.06.91.
• CHÂTEAU OF LA CHAPELLE-D'ANGILLON. 18380 La Chapelle-d'Angillon. Visits, all year round. Phone: 02.48.73.41.10.
• CHÂTEAU OF BOUCARD, 18260 Le Noyer. Visits, all year round, closed in January. Phone: 02.48.58.72.81.
• MUSÉE VASSIL-IVANOFF (VASSIL-IVANOFF MUSEUM), route des Coquilliers, 18250 La Borne. Visits, from May to mid-September, closed on Tuesdays. Phone: 02.48.26.96.24.
• MUSÉE DES POTIERS D'HIER (MUSEUM OF THE "POTTERS OF YESTERYEAR"), 18250 La Borne. Visits, on weekends, from Easter to All Saints' Day.
• CHÂTEAU OF MAUPAS, 18220 Morogues. Visits, from Palm Sunday to 15th October. Phone: 02.48.64.41.71.
• CHÂTEAU OF MENETOU-SALON, 18510 Menetou-Salon. Visits, from Easter to the end of September, closed on Tuesdays. Phone: 02.48.64.80.54.
• MUSÉE DES LAMPES À HUILE (MUSEUM OF OIL-LAMPS), 18510 Menetou-Salon.

ADDRESSES

T a b l e   o f

c o n t e n t s

Translated by David Rocher
Computer To Plate Mame Imprimeurs
© 2000 - Édilarge SA, Éditions Ouest-France
Cet ouvrage a été achevé d'imprimer
par l'imprimerie Mame à Tours (37)
N° d'éditeur : 4017.01.05.02.00 - I.S.B.N. 2.7373.2635.4
Dépôt légal : février 2000